Best Easy Day Hikes
San Luis Obispo

Help Us Keep This Guide Up to Date

Every effort has been made by the author and editors to make this guide as accurate and useful as possible. However, many things can change after a guide is published—trails are rerouted, regulations change, facilities come under new management, etc.

We would appreciate hearing from you concerning your experiences with this guide and how you feel it could be improved and kept up to date. While we may not be able to respond to all comments and suggestions, we'll take them to heart and we'll also make certain to share them with the author. Please send your comments and suggestions to the following address:

GPP
Reader Response/Editorial Department
P.O. Box 480
Guilford, CT 06437

Or you may e-mail us at:

editorial@GlobePequot.com

Thanks for your input, and happy trails!

Best Easy Day Hikes Series

Best Easy Day Hikes
San Luis Obispo

Allen Riedel

FALCONGUIDES

GUILFORD, CONNECTICUT
HELENA, MONTANA

AN IMPRINT OF GLOBE PEQUOT PRESS

FALCONGUIDES®

Copyright © 2011 by Morris Book Publishing, LLC

FalconGuides is an imprint of Globe Pequot Press.

Falcon, FalconGuides, and Outfit Your Mind are registered trademarks of Morris Book Publishing, LLC.

TOPO! Explorer software and SuperQuad source maps courtesy of National Geographic Maps. For information about TOPO! Explorer, TOPO!, and Nat Geo Maps products, go to www.topo.com or www.natgeomaps.com.

Project editor: David Legere
Layout artist: Kevin Mak
Maps created by Mapping Specialists © Morris Book Publishing, LLC.

Library of Congress Cataloging-in-Publication Data is available on file.

ISBN 978-0-7627-5116-7

Printed in the United States of America

10 9 8 7 6 5 4 3 2 1

For Sierra, Makaila, and Michael

Contents

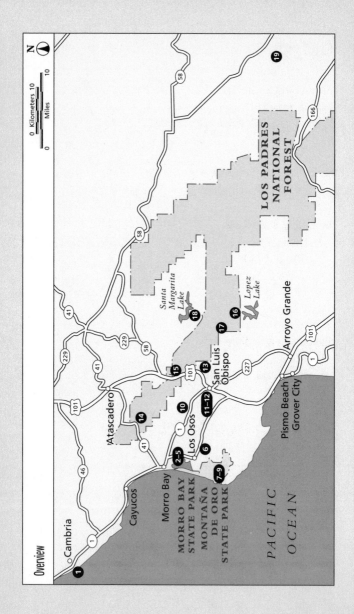

Overview

Cambria

Cayucos

Morro Bay

MORRO BAY
STATE PARK

MONTAÑA
DE ORO
STATE PARK

Los Osos

Atascadero

San Luis
Obispo

Santa
Margarita
Lake

LOS PADRES
NATIONAL
FOREST

Lopez
Lake

Arroyo Grande

Pismo Beach
Grover City

PACIFIC
OCEAN

0 Kilometers 10
0 Miles 10

N

1

2–5

6

7–9

10

11–12

13

14

15

16

17

18

19

Carrizo Plain National Monument

Acknowledgments

First and foremost, I want to thank all of the people who have spent time hiking with me in the mountains, deserts, hills, forests, jungles, and coastal beaches. Many of you, my friends, have inspired me in countless ways, and I can't thank you enough. I would like to mention some of you by name: Monique Riedel, Sean Coolican, Adam Mendelsohn, Michael Millenheft III, Sierra Riedel, Makaila Riedel, Tom Kashirsky, Cameron Alston, Matt Piazza, Bruno Lucidarme, Chrissy Ziburski, Eric Walther, Bob Romano, Jim Zuber, Danny Suarez, Dylan Riedel, Eric Romero, Donn DeBaun, Alex Wilson, Dawn Wilson, Shannon Parsons, Paul Murphy, High Kick Mike, and Jane Weal.

It is imperative and necessary and with great appreciation that I acknowledge my family: Monique, Michael, Sierra, and Makaila. All four of you have spent lots of time with me on trails that were great and some "not so much" . . . I love you with all my heart.

Thanks to my mom and dad, Barbara and Elmer Riedel, who raised me to believe in myself! Thanks to my brother, Larry; my grandparents, Herbert and Vivian Ward and Elmer and Lucille Riedel; and my in-laws, Anna and Richard Chavez. I am a better person because of all of you.

I am also grateful for the opportunities that I have been granted by writing for the most amazing website: www.localhikes.com. It seems Jim Zuber has been my biggest resource in the writing world, and I can never thank him enough for the awesome site and the amount of work he has sent my way. You rule, Jim!

I would like to thank Dave Ammenheuser and Patricia Mays at the *Press Enterprise,* who have been great editors and incredible to work for.

I would like to thank Scott Adams, John Burbidge, and the wonderful people at Globe Pequot Press, as well as my other editors, Ashley, Kate, and Carol.

Lastly, I would like to thank all of the students and teachers I have worked with over the past ten years. It has been a joy knowing all of you.

Introduction

This book contains nineteen easy day hikes situated in and around the city of San Luis Obispo, with only a couple more than an hour away from the city proper. Known to locals as simply the abbreviated San Luis, SLO, or Slo-town (pronounced *slow*), the city itself is loaded with opportunities for hiking, with most hikes suitable for the entire family. The hikes in this book are located in a variety of areas, ranging from state, county, city, and local parks to public and private lands. The book highlights the best short and easy hikes in the region.

Named for the Catholic saint Louis the Bishop, San Luis Obispo County stretches from the Santa Maria and Cuyama Rivers in the south to the 6th Standard Parallel in the north. The Temblor Range makes up the eastern border, and the graceful Pacific Ocean bounds the entire western edge. The county is fairly large, covering over 3,600 square miles—larger than Rhode Island and Delaware.

Open land is abundant throughout the county, preserving the area's pastoral and agricultural charm. The variety of scenery is quite diverse, providing many spectacular options for those looking to get outdoors and recreate. Parks, forests, beaches, mountains, and verdant rolling hills are all a part of the region's landscape. Waterfalls, lakes, year-round creeks, volcanic outcroppings, and bluff hikes are all included in this book, but the opportunities for hiking in the area are almost limitless. Resting just south of the Big Sur region, San Luis Obispo County is truly magnificent—its coastline is superbly beautiful and unique.

Aside from the luscious coastline, the morros, or Nine Sisters, of San Luis Obispo County are the area's most dominating feature. These volcanic plugs, rounded outcroppings of domes, jut forth from the earth from Morro Bay in the north to Islay Hill, just before the city of San Luis, to the south. Any traveler driving up or down the coast is sure to marvel at their picturesque splendor. Six of the nine morros can be climbed, with four of these outlined in this book. *Morro* is said to have been derived from the Spanish word for *moor,* because the rounded domes resembled the turbaned heads of Spain's Moroccan neighbors to the south.

Weather along the central coast of California is generally mild, though inland temperatures can be hot in the summer. Most summer hikes not directly on the coast are better suited for morning or evening hours. Weather patterns can and do shift, however, and the area can be socked in with fog any time of year. Rains typically fall from November through February, though generally not for long periods of time or in large amounts. Hiking and exercising in the region are popular activities, especially in the early morning and evening during summertime, and throughout the day during the fall, winter, and spring. Depending on the cloud cover and weather, summer days can be pleasant or absolutely desiccating.

Mammals abound in the mountainous regions, with larger creatures such as black bears and mule deer inhabiting the higher reaches, while mountain lions and coyotes prowl throughout most of the county. Not really presenting much of a danger, the habitat of these predators is not as threatened as in other areas of Southern California. Smaller creatures and rodents such as squirrels, skunks, possums, and mice inhabit the upper and lower coastal regions. Many species of raptors can be seen along the coast and mountain regions, including the reintroduced, though still highly endangered, California condor.

Nothing presents much of a danger except for the possibility of rattlesnakes and spiders. Do not walk through tall grasses or place hands or feet into hidden locations. Snakes are afraid of humans, and they understand the world through sensing vibrations. Typically, snakes will be alerted and flee long before a human approaches on the trail. Rattlesnakes will only strike if threatened, so the best thing to do is back away or walk in a wide berth around them on the trail.

Insects are not normally a problem in the region, though after rains ticks can be an annoyance, as can mosquitoes and other pests. Flies and gnats can be slightly troublesome in wetter areas but are not normally a nuisance. A mild insect repellent should do the trick for most hikes, and dogs should be protected with proper vaccinations and pet medicines.

Watch out for poison oak, with its three-pronged leaves. Its toxic oil, urushiol, is difficult to remove and can be spread if skin and clothing are not thoroughly cleansed after contact. Take care to avoid the plant.

Weather

San Luis Obispo County has a mostly semiarid Mediterranean climate, though coastal areas and the lower elevations can be hot but pleasant during the months of June, July, August, and September. Fog, wind, and cold can be a factor any time of year, so hikers should be prepared for quick changes in weather. Heat can also be an issue year-round, though late October through May are generally milder even in the hotter parts of the region.

Rain is not the normal state of affairs in Southern California, and San Luis is no exception, getting only between 10 and 12 inches annually. The rainy season is typically from November through February, with showers more likely during December and January. Most rainstorms are over as quickly as they begin, though the region does see periods of continuing rainfall during the winter.

Summer temperatures can reach triple digits inland, though the coastal cities rarely rise above the 80s. The best time of year to hike in and around San Luis is fall through spring, when the temperatures are mild during the day. Early morning from just before sunrise until just after sunrise and evenings from just before sunset until just after sunset are pleasant in the summer almost anywhere in the region.

Preparing for Your Hike

Before you go hiking, always be prepared. Let someone know where you are planning to go, and leave an itinerary of your hiking destination with a reliable friend. Provide an expected return time and the name of the trailhead you are visiting, along with the specific route you will be taking. Be sure that your friend will contact authorities should you not return when expected.

Water is essential. Hydrate before you leave and during your hike, and leave extra water in your vehicle so you can hydrate upon return. A good rule of thumb for hiking is one-half to one liter of water per hour of hiking, and on hot days without shade, you should drink as much as one gallon per hour of hiking. Salty snacks can help aid water retention. Avoid overexertion during the hottest part of the day.

When you hike, you should bring along the "Ten Essentials" to provide yourself with the basic necessities for survival should the unexpected occur:

1. Navigation (map, compass, GPS)
2. Sun protection (hat, sunscreen)
3. Insulation (layered clothing)
4. Illumination (head lamp, flashlight)
5. First-aid supplies (Band-Aids, bandages, gauze, tape, tweezers, etc.)
6. Repair kit and tools (knife, duct tape, etc.)
7. Nutrition (extra food)
8. Hydration (extra water)
9. Emergency shelter (tarp, tent, sleeping bag, or emergency blanket)
10. Fire starter (necessary for life-threatening emergencies only)

Hiking is a relatively safe activity, especially when care is taken, although it is always best to prepare for any eventuality. Minor mishaps, like taking a wrong turn, getting back after dark, or being lost for a short while, can be frightening, but as long as a cool head prevails, most outdoor situations can be easily rectified. The "Ten Essentials" are designed to keep people safe and provide a backup plan should something go wrong.

Other items may be fun to have along as well. Cameras can be used to record an excursion for posterity, while binoculars come in handy for wildlife viewing. Plant, bird, mammal, and insect identification guides can prove to be informative and educational. Handheld global positioning satellite (GPS) units are becoming more and more inexpensive and are a great tool to use on the trail. Maps should be taken, but most trails are well marked and maintained.

Clothing, Shoes, and Gear

Clothing should be made up of layers to protect your body from the elements, whether wind, heat, rain, or cold. An insulating layer of water- and sweat-wicking fabric (polyester, neoprene, Capilene®, or other synthetic fiber) is best for a basic layer. These fabrics wick sweat away from your body and keep you warm. On hot days cotton can be a good choice only because sweat will remain in the fabric, keeping you cooler than a synthetic material. Cotton is a bad choice for cold and rainy days, since the material retains water and loses its ability to insulate, which in extreme circumstances can lead to hypothermia.

A fleece shell is good for an insulating layer, because the material is lightweight and dries quickly. On days without a hint of precipitation, a fleece jacket may be the only outerwear needed.

Lastly, a lightweight rain shell should be brought along in case of emergencies. Rain and snow can be deadly in the mountains. A waterproof shell and pants offer protection from the elements.

Improvements in lightweight hiking boots and shoes over the past decade have revolutionized the sport. Boots no longer need to be bulky, heavy, cumbersome, Frankenstein-like appendages that cause blisters, chafing, and sore feet. Instead, many outdoor specialty shops can measure a hiker's feet and find a great-fitting shoe that can be worn immediately on the trail. These shoes are durable and sturdy and are excellent for short day hikes, though they may not be ideal for longer and more difficult trekking.

Socks made of wool or synthetic materials are best, as they pull moisture away from the feet, reducing chafing and blisters.

Backpacks for day hiking should be small, fit comfortably, and be capable of carrying ten to twenty pounds. Carrying more than twenty pounds on a day hike is actually kind of silly, and will probably only serve to make the experience less enjoyable. In today's ultralight market, weeklong backpacking trips can be made carrying only twenty to twenty-five pounds (water and food included), so find a backpack that is large enough to carry what is needed but light enough to be comfortable. Hydration systems have become the norm, and drinking from a reservoir through a tube is pure bliss compared to the days of cumbersome canteens or stopping to retrieve water bottles from a pack when thirsty.

Trail Regulations/Restrictions

Trails in this guide are located in national forests, preserves, and local and regional parks. Some trails pass through private property. As of this writing, access is allowed in these areas, but care should be taken not to abuse this privilege. Be careful and courteous, and always respect private property. Landowners can shut off access to their property if unsightly trash and negative behaviors become the norm. Do your part to protect these refuges.

Some city parks and natural areas are free, while others require day-use fees. Fees for trailhead usage are not required anywhere, though camping permits may carry fees.

Play It Safe

Generally, hiking in and around the San Luis Obispo region is a safe and fun way to explore the outdoors. Hiking is not without its risks, but there are ways to lessen those risks. Following a few simple steps and guidelines will help to make the activity as benign as possible:

- It is a good idea to know simple first aid, including how to treat bleeding, bites and stings, and fractures, strains, or sprains. Be sure to take along at least a basic first-aid kit. It won't help to have the skills without any supplies.

- San Luis, and all of Southern California for that matter, is known for its sunny skies and warm climate. The sun can be powerful, especially at higher elevations; use sunscreen and wear a wide-brimmed hat. Weather patterns can change abruptly. Carry the proper layers of clothing to protect you from temperature changes and rain.

- Rattlesnakes may be found on any of the hikes described, particularly from early spring to mid-fall. Be careful where you place your hands and feet.

- Learn how to spot and identify poison oak. Its appearance will change throughout the year. During spring and summer the distinctive three-pronged leaf may appear green and then turn to red and brown as the season progresses into winter. In winter the leaves may completely fall off the plant, leaving a hard-to-identify stalk that still contains and spreads the toxins when touched. The noxious plant grows abundantly near water, in the canyons, and along the hillsides.

- Ticks are another pest to be avoided. They are more likely to be found near water or after rains, and hang in the brush waiting to drop on warm-blooded animals. It is a good idea to check for ticks whenever pausing along the trail. Ticks will generally hang on to clothing or hair and not bite until the host has stopped moving. Remove them before they have a chance to bite.

Etiquette

There really aren't any rules for hiking, other than those outlined by specific parks and agencies that govern each parcel of land, but there are a few unwritten guidelines to follow. Mostly they are common sense, but some are not always intuitive. Right of way on the trail is always as follows: equestrians first, pedestrians next, and then bicyclists. Hikers and bicyclists must always yield to horses, and bicyclists must always yield to hikers.

While it isn't necessarily written, the courteous thing to do on the trail is to always yield to uphill hikers. Hiking uphill is harder and more taxing; when walking uphill hikers get into a rhythm, and making them stop is just plain rude. However, those hiking uphill will often stop to let downhill hikers pass simply to get a rest. If you are hiking downhill and you notice the people coming your way have some serious mojo going, let them continue. It is a lot easier getting started going down. Of course, common sense should also rule the day; backpackers carrying heavy loads on narrow trails might need hikers going uphill to step aside, and equestrian users may find a suitable space to stop before a hiker even comes close to them.

When hiking with dogs, always bring a leash. Even if there is no requirement that a dog be leashed, some people are afraid of dogs and it is courteous to leash dogs up when others approach. Unruly and vicious dogs are better left at home, as dog owners are legally liable for any damage their pets may cause. Make sure your pet is trained when off leash so that it will not disturb or harass wildlife or others.

Zero Impact

Trails in the San Luis area are used year-round. We, as trail users and advocates, must be especially vigilant to make sure our passage leaves no lasting mark. Here are some basic guidelines for preserving trails in the region:

- Pack out all your own trash, including biodegradable items like orange peels and sunflower seeds. In the arid Southern California climate, items such as these take ten or more years to decompose. If everyone who hiked these trails left peels and shells behind, the trails would look more like a waste dump than a forest or wild landscape. You might also pack out garbage left by less considerate hikers—take a plastic bag and make the place better for your having been there.

- Don't approach or feed any wild creatures—the ground squirrel eyeing your snack food is best able to survive if it remains self-reliant.

- Don't pick wildflowers or gather rocks, antlers, feathers, or other treasures along the trail. Removing these items will only take away from the next hiker's experience.

- Avoid damaging trailside soils and plants by remaining on the established route. This is also a good rule of thumb for avoiding poison oak and stinging nettle, common regional trailside irritants.

- Don't cut switchbacks, which can promote erosion.

- Be courteous by not making loud noises while hiking.
- Many of these trails are multiuse, which means you'll share them with other hikers, trail runners, mountain bikers, and equestrians. Familiarize yourself with the proper trail etiquette, yielding the trail when appropriate.
- Use outhouses at trailheads or along the trail.
- Be respectful of private property rights.

The Falcon Zero-Impact Principles

- Leave with everything you brought with you.
- Leave no sign of your visit.
- Leave the landscape as you found it.

How to Use This Guide

This guide is designed to be simple and easy to use. Each hike is described with a map and summary information that delivers the trail's vital statistics including distance, approximate hiking time, elevation gain, difficulty, trail surface, best season, other trail users, canine compatibility, fees and permits, and trail contacts. Directions to the trailhead from San Luis Obispo are also provided, along with a general description of what you'll see along the way. A detailed route finder (Miles and Directions) sets forth mileages between significant landmarks along the trail.

Maps

Easy to follow maps are provided for each hike. All the hikes in this book are covered by Topo! CD: California CD 9 and the detailed topographic maps published by the U.S. Geological Survey (USGS).

Hike Selection

The hikes listed in this book range from leisurely strolls to more challenging hikes. You will find hikes that range in distance from about 1.0 mile to 7.0 miles, across varying terrain. Whether you are visiting for a weekend, or a local of many years, you should find a hike in this book to serve your interests. There are excellent options for getting a good workout, as well as options that are best for days when you just want to get outside without too much effort. It is important to remember that while we believe these are the best easy day hikes in the area, not every hike is right for every person. Read the hike descriptions to help you choose the right hike for you and your hiking partners.

Difficulty Ratings

These are all easy hikes, but easy is a relative term. A fit runner may find a 3.0-mile, hilly hike easy, while some may expect easy to be short and flat. First-time hikers and seasoned veterans likely also have different expectations. So to aid in the selection of a hike that suits your particular needs and abilities, each hike is rated easy, moderate, or more challenging. Bear in mind that even the most challenging routes can be made easy by hiking within your limits and taking rests when you need them.

- **Easy** hikes are generally short and/or have little elevation gain, usually taking no more than an hour to complete.
- **Moderate** hikes involve more elevation gain, and may require slightly more coordination than the easy hikes, often crossing streams or scrambling over rocks.
- **More challenging** hikes feature some steep stretches, greater distances, and generally require more fitness and technical skills.

These are completely subjective ratings—consider that what you think is easy is entirely dependent on your level of fitness and coordination, and the adequacy of your gear. If you are hiking with a group, you should select a hike with a rating that's appropriate for the least fit and prepared in your party.

Approximate hiking times are based on the assumption that on flat ground, most walkers average 2 to 3 miles per hour. Adjust that rate by the steepness of the terrain and your level of fitness (subtract time if you're an aerobic animal and add time if you're hiking with kids), and you have a ballpark hiking duration. Be sure to add more time if you plan to picnic or take part in other activities like bird watching or photography. It is also important to note that a hiking trip does not only entail moving time. Plan more time if you tend to take a lot of pictures, or stop to frequently take in views.

Map Legend

══🛡101🛡══	U.S. Highway
══🛡1🛡══	State Highway
———	Local Road
= = = = = =	Unpaved Road
▬▬▬▬▬▬	Featured Trail
- - - - - -	Trail
~~	River/Creek
░░░	Sand
~~	Marsh
⬭	Body of Water
▬ ▬ ▬	State or Local Park/Preserve
▬ ▬ ▬	National Forest
⋀	Camping
▭	Inn
▲	Mountain Peak
🅿	Parking
㋡	Picnic Area
■	Point of Interest/Structure
🚻	Restroom
○	Town
❶	Trailhead
◐	Viewpoint/Overlook
❓	Visitor/Information Center
⋙	Waterfall

Fiscalini Ranch Preserve

Originally, the land now known as the Fiscalini Ranch Preserve was inhabited by the Chumash Indians. With Spanish settlement it became part of the Rancho Santa Rosa Land Grant and eventually was owned by the Phelan family as a parcel of the massive Phelan Ranch. The region has gone by many names, including one that still gets quite a bit of usage, East-West Ranch.

This land was eventually preserved and protected by a dedicated group of citizens fighting under different names, including Friends of Ranchland, Small Wilderness Area Preservation (SWAP) with the help of the American Land Conservancy, the State Coastal Conservancy, local government, and Mid State Bank. The Cambria Community Services District holds the title on the property, and the Friends of Fiscalini Ranch will eventually gain all access and rights to control and manage the property.

The Fiscalini Ranch Preserve is nearly 1.0 mile in length and borders a breathtaking bluff system along the Pacific Ocean. It also incorporates a part of Santa Rosa Creek and is critical habitat for endangered species such as red-legged frogs, tidewater gobies, and Monterey pines.

1   Fiscalini Ranch Preserve

Stroll along lovely beachside bluffs, perfect for enjoying wildlife or watching the sunset.

Distance: 4.05-mile lollipop
Approximate hiking time: 2 hours
Elevation gain: 300 feet
Difficulty: Easy
Trail surface: Dirt, rock, boardwalk
Best season: Year-round

Other trail users: Dogs, bikes
Canine compatibility: Leashed dogs allowed
Fees and permits: None
Trail contact: Friends of Fiscalini Ranch, P.O. Box 1664, Cambria, CA 93428; (805) 927-2856

Finding the trailhead: From the intersection of Marsh and Higuera Streets, head west onto US 101 North and drive for 1.4 miles. Take the California Boulevard exit, turn right onto California Boulevard, and drive for 0.5 mile. Turn left onto East Foothill Boulevard and drive for 0.2 mile. Turn right onto CA 1 North/Cabrillo Highway/North Santa Rosa Street and drive for 33.6 miles. Turn left onto Windsor Boulevard and drive for 0.4 mile. Turn right onto Bristol Street and continue as it curves and turns into Nottingham Drive for 0.3 mile. Nottingham also curves and becomes Huntington Drive. Continue onto Huntington Drive for 0.3 mile and park. GPS Trailhead Coordinates: 35° 33' 43" N, -121° 06' 07" W

The Hike

From the parking area on Huntington Drive, walk south into Fiscalini Ranch on the Ridge Trail. While the sounds of CA 1 are never far off, the open grassland and striking views of the ocean give this 400 acres of coastal splendor a

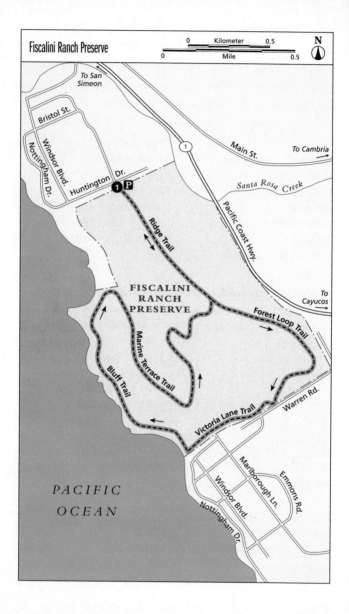

feeling of true remoteness. Walk for 0.5 mile and approach a four-way intersection of trails. Take the trail to the left and continue into a grove of Monterey pine, oak, and eucalyptus. At 0.75 mile take the left fork again and merge onto the Forest Loop Trail. Here you can fully appreciate the beauty of the woodlands in the region. This ecosystem is truly a treasure and the region is lucky to have had it preserved. The Monterey pines are breathtaking, and it is difficult to imagine anyone conceiving that this area should have been a strip mall and tract housing. Here the highway seems farther off, and it is quite tranquil.

At 1.25 miles connect with the Victoria Lane Trail and follow it as it eventually meets with the developed and boardwalked Marine Terrace Trail at 1.5 miles. Take the patchwork system of small trails toward the ocean and connect onto the breathtaking Bluff Trail at 1.6 miles. This is the most stunning part of the hike. Towering cliffs stand above the gentle Pacific, and this is a great place for a sunset stroll.

The Big Sur region of California sits just to the north of Cambria, and the coastal portion of this hike is as beautiful as any along that storied coastline. Follow the Bluff Trail north along the coastline and meet up with the Marine Terrace Trail. As you walk, enjoy any one of the unique benches provided for those who wish to take in a relaxing ocean view. The Marine Terrace Trail provides access to all so that everyone, including those with physical disabilities, can enjoy the serenity and beauty of the preserve. At 3.0 miles turn left and take the Terrace to Ridge Trail back to the Ridge Trail. Make another left at 3.5 miles and take the middle trail at 3.55 miles, when the route returns to the same four-way crossing encountered near the beginning of the hike. Walk the remaining 0.5 mile back to Nottingham Drive.

Disabled visitors wishing to access only the boardwalk portion of the trail can park at the end of South Windsor Boulevard. Interpretive signs line the route nearer the coast and provide lots of detail about the natural history and ecology of the preserve.

Miles and Directions

0.0 From Huntington Drive walk south along the Ridge Trail.

0.5 Turn left at the four-way trail crossing and head toward the Forest Loop Trail.

0.75 Turn left onto the Forest Loop Trail.

1.25 Connect with the Victoria Lane Trail and follow it southwest toward the coast.

1.5 Cross the Marine Terrace Trail. Follow the network of use trails toward the coast and Bluff Trail.

1.6 Head northwest along the Bluff Trail and follow it to its completion and connection with the Marine Terrace Trail.

2.5 Continue back southeast along the Marine Terrace Trail boardwalk.

3.0 Turn left onto the Terrace to Ridge Trail.

3.5 Turn left.

3.55 Take the middle trail (Ridge Trail) at the four-way junction.

4.05 Arrive back at Huntington Drive.

Morro Bay State Park

Morro Bay State Park is a highly developed yet peaceful preserve with an irregular balance between its natural aesthetics and the recreational/modern improvements of the park. The park contains a marina, a museum of natural history, a developed campground complete with showers and RV hookups, and a golf course. Alongside these man-made additions, there exists a natural world full of beauty and wonder.

Both Chorro and Los Osos Creeks flow into Morro Bay from the higher mountain reaches of the county, while two of the nine morros of San Luis Obispo County are protected within the confines of the park. Cerro Cabrillo and Black Hill can both be climbed, while the sacred Morro Rock is nearly omnipresent sitting majestically off to the northwest in the calm Pacific. The Morro Estuary is a natural preserve protecting the coastal wetlands and the biodiversity of the region. Many trails wander through the park, some much more wild than others. The trip to Cerro Cabrillo is a lovely little underutilized trail, while the trip to Black Hill is a bit more mechanized and easier to access.

Also under the auspices of park control are the El Moro Elfin Preserve and the Los Osos Oaks State Reserve, two wonderfully unique ecosystems that demonstrate the area's diversity and splendor. People visiting from late October through late January may want to check out the migrating monarch butterflies that nest and roost near campground 116.

2 Black Hill

Take a short hike to the top of a volcanic plug dome and enjoy exquisite views of Morro Bay and the Central Coast.

Distance: 1.6 miles out and back

Approximate hiking time: 1 hour

Elevation gain: 550 feet

Difficulty: Easy

Trail surface: Dirt and sand

Best season: Year-round

Other trail users: None

Canine compatibility: Dogs not permitted

Fees and permits: Day-use fee per vehicle

Trail contact: Morro Bay State Park, State Park Road, Morro Bay, CA 93442; (805) 772-7434

Finding the trailhead: From the intersection of Marsh and Higuera Streets, head west on Marsh, taking the ramp onto US 101 North. Drive for 1.4 miles to the California Boulevard exit. Turn right and take California Boulevard for 0.5 mile. Turn left onto East Foothill Boulevard and drive for 0.2 mile. Turn right onto CA 1 North/Cabrillo Highway/North Santa Rosa Street and drive for 10.4 miles. Exit at Los Osos/Baywood Park. Turn left onto South Bay Boulevard and drive for 0.7 mile. Turn right onto State Park Road and drive for 0.1 mile, veering right at the fork. Continue 0.3 mile to the turnout on the right and park. GPS Trailhead Coordinates: 35° 21' 05" N, -120° 50' 01" W

The Hike

Of the nine morros located throughout San Luis Obispo County (often referred to as the Nine Sisters), Black Hill is the second-to-last volcanic plug before Morro Rock and the easiest of the peaks to summit. Park alongside the roadway and walk westward on Lower State Park Road for 0.05 mile. The trail meets the road and branches north and up toward Black Hill and south toward the estuary. Take a right turn onto the unsigned path and head uphill toward a grove of eucalyptus trees. The trail climbs softly as it meanders through a peaceful hollow before meeting an unsigned trail junction at 0.4 mile. Veer left and continue up toward Black Hill. Here among the towering eucalyptus remain some old buildings and a residual water tower. The trail begins to wind below the peak and is nicely shaded under a peaceful arbor.

At this point the trail meets several use paths that enter onto the main trail from the left along Upper State Park Road/Black Hill Road. Stay right and on the main trail as it begins to curve around the base of the summit. The trail nears a water-storage unit and meets the end of Upper State Park Road/Black Hill Road. At 0.6 mile turn right behind the kiosk and walk the remaining 0.2 mile up the hill. From here the views open up back into the estuary and Montana de Oro State Park, over the town of Morro Bay, out into the Pacific Ocean, and inland along the spines of the closest of the nine morros, Cerro Cabrillo and Hollister Peak.

The summit is spectacular at both sunset and sunrise. Migrating birds fly over and help to make the top of Black Hill a cozy little place for a respite and a snack.

Those wishing to make this an even easier hike can park at the top of Upper Park State Road/Black Hill Road and simply ascend the 0.2 mile to the top without even breaking a sweat.

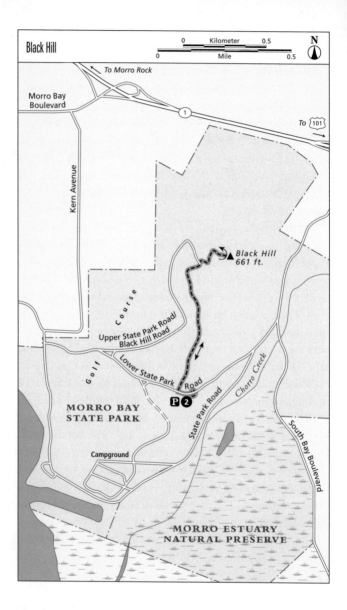

Kilometer
0   0.5
Mile
0   0.5

N

To Morro Rock

Morro Bay
Boulevard

1

To 101

Kern Avenue

Golf   Course

Upper State Park Road/
Black Hill Road

Lower State Park   Road

State Park Road

Chorro Creek

South Bay Boulevard

Black Hill
661 ft.

P 2

MORRO BAY
STATE PARK

Campground

MORRO ESTUARY
NATURAL PRESERVE

Miles and Directions

0.0 Walk west along Lower State Park Road.

0.05 Turn right onto the unsigned trail heading up toward Black Hill.

0.4 Veer left at the trail junction and follow the trail around the base of the summit.

0.6 Intersect with Upper State Park Road/Black Hill Road. Turn right and follow the trail up to the top.

0.8 Arrive on the summit of Black Hill. Return via the same route.

1.6 Arrive back at the parking area.

3 Windy Cove

Enjoy a family stroll along a semi–secluded harbor, savoring coastal views of the harbor, wonderful eucalyptus groves, and some natural history.

Distance: 0.8 mile out and back
Approximate hiking time: 1 hour
Elevation gain: 10 feet
Difficulty: Easy
Trail surface: Dirt and sand
Best season: Year-round
Other trail users: None

Canine compatibility: Dogs not permitted
Fees and permits: Day-use fee per vehicle
Trail contact: Morro Bay State Park, State Park Road, Morro Bay, CA 93442; (805) 772-7434

Finding the trailhead: From the intersection of Marsh and Higuera Streets, head west on Marsh, taking the ramp onto US 101 North. Drive for 1.4 miles to the California Boulevard exit. Turn right and take California Boulevard for 0.5 mile. Turn left onto East Foothill Boulevard and drive for 0.2 mile. Turn right onto CA 1 North/Cabrillo Highway/North Santa Rosa Street and drive for 10.4 miles. Exit at Los Osos/Baywood Park. Turn left onto South Bay Boulevard and drive for 0.7 mile. Turn right onto State Park Road and drive for 0.1 mile, continuing left on State Park Road at the fork. Drive for 1.1 miles. Turn left and park in the museum parking lot. GPS Trailhead Coordinates: 35° 20' 50" N, -120° 50' 39" W

The Hike

From the Natural History Museum in Morro Bay State Park, walk north along the coast and harbor. A beautiful sandy beach looks out onto the mingling freshwaters of

Chorro and Los Osos Creeks that mix and churn with the salty waters of the Pacific in the Morro Estuary Natural Preserve, the largest protected estuary in the state. Eight hundred acres shield rookeries and bird habitat that are home to over one hundred migrating species in the winter. The estuary is an important part of the Pacific Flyway and a great place for birdwatching.

Follow the dirt path that strolls gently and flatly below tall eucalyptus trees. Along the way visitors will find some interpretive signs that teach about the ecology of the region. Those looking north can see the towering monolith of Morro Rock and the three 450-foot-tall giant smokestacks that form the Duke Energy electrical plant, built in 1954. The scenery is idyllic, and even though the park road skirts almost the entire route, the cove emanates a wonderful feeling of serenity. The boats floating on Morro Bay, the sand spit stretching from Morro Rock to Montana de Oro State Park, and the blue skies combine to make this a fantastic area for photography. The hike can be done with volunteer docents, who can answer just about any question dreamt of in regard to the region and its ecosystems. Check at the front desk of the museum for a schedule and to sign up for the interactive walk, which is sure to be fascinating for children and adults alike.

There really isn't a right or wrong way to do this walk. Children may want to play along the shore, while couples may wish to stroll, casually taking in the sights and sounds. Those wishing to walk the 0.4 mile to the Inn at Morro Bay can do so and then turn around and return to the parking area. Those who wish to make the turnaround sooner can also do so.

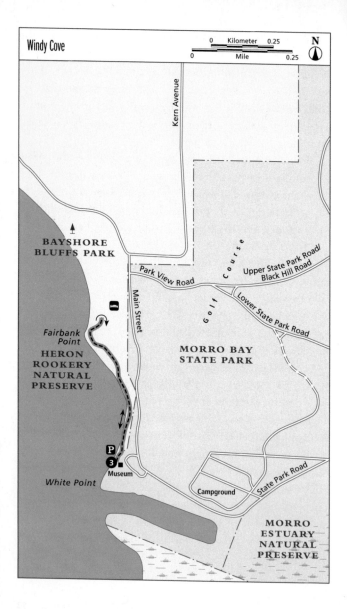

Windy Cove

0   Kilometer   0.25
0   Mile   0.25

N

Kern Avenue

BAYSHORE
BLUFFS PARK

Park View Road

Golf Course

Upper State Park Road/
Black Hill Road

Lower State Park Road

Main Street

Fairbank
Point

HERON
ROOKERY
NATURAL
PRESERVE

MORRO BAY
STATE PARK

P
3
Museum

White Point

Campground

State Park Road

MORRO
ESTUARY
NATURAL
PRESERVE

Windy Cove is appropriately named—visitors will want to bring along a light jacket as the chill from the gusting breezes can get downright frigid at times.

Miles and Directions

0.0 From the Natural History Museum, walk north along the path through Windy Cove.

0.4 Reach the Inn at Morro Bay and return via the same route.

0.8 Arrive back at the Natural History Museum.

4 Cerro Cabrillo/Cabrillo Peak

Climb to the top of one of San Luis Obispo's nine morros and gain overpowering views of the Pacific Coast, Morro Bay, and its estuary.

Distance: 3.0 miles out and back

Approximate hiking time: 1.5 hours

Elevation gain: 900 feet

Difficulty: Moderate

Trail surface: Dirt

Best season: Year-round

Other trail users: None

Canine compatibility: Dogs not permitted

Fees and permits: No fees or permits required

Trail contact: Morro Bay State Park, State Park Road, Morro Bay, CA 93442; (805) 772-7434

Finding the trailhead: From the intersection of Marsh and Higuera Streets, head west on Marsh, taking the ramp onto US 101 North. Drive for 1.4 miles to the California Boulevard exit. Turn right and take California Boulevard for 0.5 mile. Turn left onto East Foothill Boulevard and drive for 0.2 mile. Turn right onto CA 1 North/Cabrillo Highway/North Santa Rosa Street and drive for 10.4 miles. Exit at Los Osos/Baywood Park. Turn left onto South Bay Boulevard and drive for 1.4 miles. Turn left and park in the trailhead parking lot. GPS Trailhead Coordinates: 35° 20' 49" N, -120° 49' 32" W

The Hike

Cerro Cabrillo (Cabrillo Peak) is the third volcanic plug dome from Morro Rock. The entire peak rests within Morro Bay State Park, and at 911 feet it provides breathtaking views of Morro Bay, its estuary, Hollister Peak, and the Pacific coastline. The trail does gain elevation rather rapidly when ascending to the peak, but generally those in fairly decent shape should find the trip exhilarating and easily doable. It makes for a great training hike because of the quick elevation gain and relatively short distance from beginning to end.

From the parking lot on South Bay Boulevard, head northeast along the trail, which follows the remnants of some old dirt roads that used to make their way to quarries around the morro. For the first 0.25 mile, the route climbs 200 feet above the coastal plain, passes the old quarry site, and then settles into a plateau for the next 0.5 mile. Here the trail meanders gently through coastal chaparral and scrub. The route is wide and easy. Some views can be had from this point of the estuary and Black Hill.

At 0.75 mile the trail branches. Turn left and head north toward the summit. Here the route becomes quite steep and gains over 500 feet in elevation in a little more than a quarter of a mile. The large standing rock outcroppings are called tikis because they resemble Polynesian statues. Keep climbing upward, as this push takes the hiker to the upper reaches of the peak, providing absolutely breathtaking views. The summit is just ahead at a little over 1.0 mile in total distance from the beginning of the hike.

The top of Cerro Cabrillo is a half-mile-long hogback that should be explored from end to end for the varying perspective of views that it provides. Hikers return via the same route.

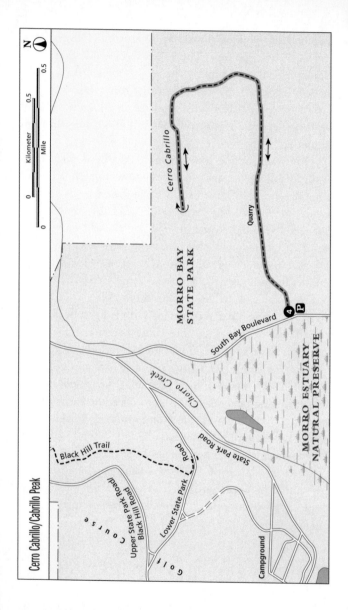

Cerro Cabrillo/Cabrillo Peak

Miles and Directions

0.0 From the parking lot, hike northeast along the trail.

0.75 Turn left and climb up Cerro Cabrillo.

1.1 Reach the high point.

1.5 Reach the western high point. Turn around. Return via the same route.

3.0 Arrive back at the parking area.

5 El Moro Elfin Forest

Take a trip through a miniature forest along the central California coast and enjoy a unique wetland ecosystem.

Distance: 1.1-mile lollipop
Approximate hiking time: 1 hour
Elevation gain: 100 feet
Difficulty: Easy
Trail surface: Boardwalk
Best season: Year-round
Other trail users: Dogs

Canine compatibility: Leashed dogs permitted
Fees and permits: None
Trail contact: Small Wilderness Area Preservation (SWAP), PO Box 6442, Los Osos, CA 93412; (805) 528-0392

Finding the trailhead: From the intersection of Marsh and Higuera Streets, head west on Marsh under the US 101 freeway, taking the ramp onto US 101 South. Drive for 0.2 mile and exit at CA 227/Madonna Road. Turn left onto Madonna Road and drive for 1.0 mile. Make a right onto Los Osos Valley Road and drive for 8.7 miles. Turn right onto South Bay Boulevard. Drive for 1.5 miles. Turn left onto Santa Ysabel Avenue and drive for 0.1 mile. Make a right turn onto 16th Street and park at the end of the road. Disabled parking is available. GPS Trailhead Coordinates: 35° 19' 54" N, -120° 49' 31" W

The Hike

While the El Moro Elfin Forest is not entirely unique—certainly other wetlands harbor "elfin forests"—there are subspecies of plants that grow here that are found nowhere else on the planet, and its semi-secluded locale makes the preserve appear otherworldly. The name is a lighthearted take on the size of some of the diminutive plants, specifically the oak trees, which grow in miniature due to the extremes in climate and salinity. The preserve has periods of drought and flooding with both salt and fresh water, so all of the species have adapted to this environment and thrive here. The plants can survive both the winter periods of saltwater flooding and the arid extremes of the desertlike summer. The whole family will enjoy a trip to the Elfin Forest, and the route described here follows the boardwalk through the preserve and is accessible to visitors with disabilities. Intermittently, the boardwalk has placards nailed to the outside baseboards that identify plants and stops along the brochure-guided interpretive trail. Large informational signs are also present in deck areas and overlooks.

From 16th Street, walk north into the preserve. The trip begins by passing through a coastal dune scrub environment filled with black sage and California sagebrush. Quickly the trail enters into a maritime chaparral community filled with chamise and buckbrush. In less than 0.1 mile, the trail ends at a T-junction. Turn right and follow the main boardwalk route along the Ridge Trail as it curves north making a loop. In the next 0.1 mile, three smaller trails enter from the right—keep left to stay on the main route as it joins with the Celestial Meadow Trail. Here the trail enters and skirts along miniature coast live oaks. On the left the trail joins Rose Bowker Grove (formerly Wood Rat Hall). As of October 2009, visitors can now walk under the pygmy oaks via the newly constructed boardwalk and decking. Those with a discerning eye can spot the complex creations of sticks and debris left behind by the forest's resident rodents in the underbrush.

At 0.4 mile turn right and follow the route 0.07 mile to an overlook of the salt marsh and the Pacific Ocean from

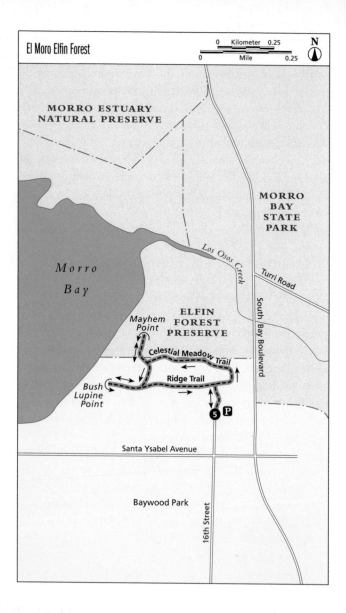

Mayhem Point. Return back to the main trail and turn right. At 0.6 mile turn right again to head toward the ocean for another vantage view from Bush Lupine Point at 0.7 mile. Return to the main Ridge Trail and continue back to the turnoff for 16th Street where the hike began.

Miles and Directions

0.0 From 16th Street walk north into the preserve.

0.07 Turn right at the T-junction, staying on the boardwalk loop.

0.2 Reach Rose Bowker Grove/Wood Rat Hall.

0.4 Turn right and follow the boardwalk to Mayhem Point Overlook.

0.47 Reach Mayhem Point. Return to the main loop.

0.55 Arrive at the main loop and turn right.

0.6 Veer right, following the boardwalk to Bush Lupine Point.

0.7 Arrive at Bush Lupine Point. Return to the main loop.

0.8 Veer right, staying on the Ridge Trail.

1.03 Arrive at the 16th Street junction and turn right.

1.1 Arrive back at the parking lot on 16th Street.

6 Los Osos Oaks State Reserve

Take a walk through a lovely grove of ancient pygmy oaks, enjoying the shade of a magical arbor.

Distance: 1.1-mile lollipop
Approximate hiking time: 1 hour
Elevation gain: 75 feet
Difficulty: Easy
Trail surface: Dirt
Best season: Year-round
Other trail users: None

Canine compatibility: Dogs not permitted
Fees and permits: None
Trail contact: Los Osos Oaks State Reserve, c/o Morro Bay State Park, State Park Road, Morro Bay, CA 93442; (805) 772-7434

Finding the trailhead: From the intersection of Marsh and Higuera Streets, head west on Marsh under the US 101 freeway, taking the ramp onto US 101 South. Drive for 0.2 mile and exit at CA 227/Madonna Road. Turn left onto Madonna Road and drive for 1.0 mile. Make a right onto Los Osos Valley Road and drive for 8.0 miles. Turn left into the parking area for Los Osos Oaks. GPS Trailhead Coordinates: 35° 18' 22" N, -120° 48' 49" W

The Hike

Los Osos means "the bears" in Spanish. It was so named due to the grizzly bears that once flourished in the area. Local rumor has it that the Spaniards in Gaspar de Portola's Alta California expedition who happened upon the region saw hundreds of the creatures grazing and roaming about the valley.

Similar to the El Moro Elfin Preserve, the pygmy oaks protected at Los Osos Oaks State Reserve are a remnant of ancient coastal ecosystems that have largely vanished due to human activity and development. From the time of the Spanish era of Mexican land grants, most of the surrounding valley was cleared for grazing and agriculture. Once highly abundant along the California coastline, this is one of the last surviving pygmy oak woodlands and certainly the largest. Though not really feasible to become "lost" in the preserve, it certainly feels possible. In other areas of California, similar ancient sand dune ecosystems were developed into communities and housing projects. The pygmy oaks, like the grizzly bear, were all but extinguished, but surprisingly this grove was spared from all development and eventually saved by SWAP (Small Wilderness Area Preservation) in 1971.

Walk west through the parking lot to the trailhead, following the route as it curves left and enters into the woodlands almost immediately. Near the start of the trail, noise from the busy boulevard of Los Osos Valley Road permeates, but after a short amount of walking, the preserve becomes peaceful and the city and its traffic seem worlds away. At 0.08 mile the trail comes to a four-way junction. Turn right and follow the Chumash Loop. The pygmy oaks are wondrous, twisting and bending overhead and through the underbrush. They are extraordinarily beautiful, and the 90-acre park is surprisingly peaceful. Lichen and moss hang from the trees like some kind of mysterious outdoor decoration.

The trail is very gentle and flat and is a great place for families to come and stretch their legs. Poison oak is ubiquitous, however, so it is important to remain vigilant and watchful throughout. Those with small children should be especially careful. At 0.3 mile the trail branches with another junction. Turn right again and follow the Oak View Trail as

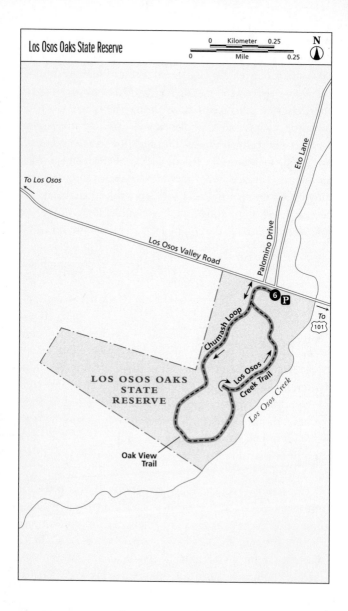

Los Osos Oaks State Reserve

Kilometer
0   0.25
Mile
0   0.25

N

To Los Osos

Eto Lane

Palomino Drive

Los Osos Valley Road

6 P

To 101

Chumash Loop

LOS OSOS OAKS
STATE
RESERVE

Los Osos

Creek Trail

Los Osos Creek

Oak View
Trail

it loops through the southernmost reaches of the preserve. At times along the ridge, views open up east toward the city of San Luis Obispo and several of the morros that dot the landscape of the region. At 0.7 mile turn right again and follow the outside loop of the Los Osos Creek Trail. Here the route borders along some riparian woodland, and running water can be present throughout the year, though not normally during the dry season of summer. At just over a mile, the trail reaches the same four-way junction. Turn right again and return to the parking area.

Miles and Directions

0.0   From the parking area walk west to the trailhead.

0.08 Turn right at the trail crossing/four-way junction. Follow the Chumash Loop Trail.

0.3   At the junction turn right onto the Oak View Trail.

0.7   Turn right onto the Los Osos Creek Trail.

1.02 Turn right at the four-way junction.

1.1   Arrive back at the parking area.

Montana de Oro
State Park

Montana de Oro State Park is a shining gem of the California State Park system. It is remarkably beautiful, not highly developed, not overly used, and relatively still a secret among the vast beauty of California. Sitting 7.0 miles away from the center of the town of Los Osos, driving to the park feels almost like taking a voyage off into a remote wilderness forgotten by humanity and time, and quite frankly those who do not know of the park's existence won't just happen upon it. For those who do come here, it becomes a favorite, and most return time and time again.

The park is comprised of 8,000 acres of unspoiled coastal beauty. In fact, its 7.0 miles of shoreline makes it one of the largest undeveloped coastal regions in California. Its name, Montana de Oro, means mountain of gold, and anyone that visits in the spring will know why. The wildflowers that bloom are mostly of a beautiful yellow coloring. Hills are often covered with California poppies, but also common are outcroppings of arroyo lupine, hummingbird sage, Johnny-jump-ups, purple nightshade, sticky monkey flower, rush-rose, and meadow rue. Bluffs, mountains, creeks, inlets, tide pools, and canyons make up the park's majesty, and even the sand spit that stretches from Morro Bay to Hazard Canyon is included in the park's boundary. Raptors and other birds can be seen lofting by on the ocean updrafts. Camping, fishing, hiking, and cycling are all possible in Montana de Oro, though RVs longer than 27 feet are not allowed on the road into the park.

While hiking in Montana de Oro, there is a feeling that California has returned to an age before the Spanish explorers, an era when cities and traffic didn't exist. It is possible to hike and not see any trace of the footprint of humanity. The area feels as remote as it is, and for California coastline, that is quite special.

7 Hazard Peak

Take a summit hike to wonderful views of the surrounding vicinity from Morro Bay to San Luis Obispo.

Distance: 3.5 miles out and back

Approximate hiking time: 2 hours

Elevation gain: 930 feet

Difficulty: Moderate

Trail surface: Dirt and sand

Best season: Year-round

Other trail users: None

Canine compatibility: Dogs not permitted

Fees and permits: None

Trail contact: Montana de Oro State Park, 1 Pecho Valley Road, Los Osos, CA 93402; (805) 528-0513 or (805) 772-7434

Finding the trailhead: From the intersection of Marsh and Higuera Streets, head west on Marsh under the US 101 freeway, taking the ramp onto US 101 South. Drive for 0.2 mile and exit at CA 227/Madonna Road. Turn left onto Madonna Road and drive for 1.0 mile. Make a right onto Los Osos Valley Road and drive for 10.3 miles. Continue on Pecho Valley Road for 3.3 miles. Park at the Ridge Trailhead. GPS trailhead Coordinates: 35° 16' 38" N, -120° 53' 06" W

The Hike

Hazard Peak is perhaps the easiest summit in all of Montana de Oro State Park. The climb itself is steady and gentle, while the total elevation gain is just under 1,000 feet. The trip to the peak measures in at just below 2.0 miles, and while the tip isn't as high as Valencia, Oats, or Alan Peaks, the views are nearly as exquisite, and the required work in getting to the top isn't nearly as difficult. Since the entirety of Morro Bay and the sand spit can be seen from the apex,

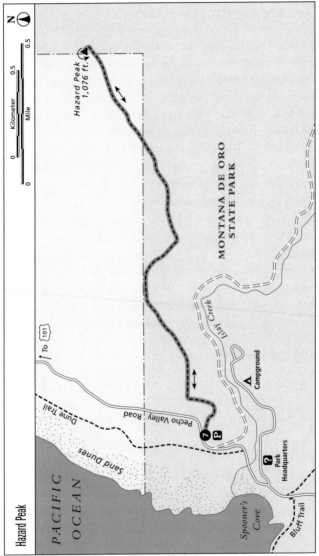

Hazard Peak

some people prefer this hike to other summits in the park. To be certain, the views are quite stellar.

Since Hazard Peak sits in front of the other higher peaks in the region and closer to the ocean, the views of the coastline and Morro Bay are unobstructed. Eight of the nine morros of San Luis Obispo County can be seen from the top, making Hazard Peak an outstanding as well as relatively easy destination for hikers of all abilities.

From the Ridge Trail/Hazard Peak trailhead parking lot, head east up the trail. The ascent is fairly gentle for a peak, but it still gains 500 feet of elevation in a mile, which isn't necessarily a cakewalk. However, it is decidedly doable for anyone with the ability to walk over a few miles. Gaining the remaining 500 feet is a bit steeper and is accomplished in just under 0.75 mile. Views begin to open up almost immediately, though the best are to be had from the summit. It is possible to make this hike into a longer loop, but most hikers will be satisfied with the views from the summit and return the way they came.

Miles and Directions

0.0 From the parking area for the Ridge Trail, head east on the Ridge Trail.

1.75 Reach the summit of Hazard Peak. Return via the same route.

3.5 Arrive back at the parking area.

8 Bluff Trail

Hike along breathtaking bluffs and marvel in the beauty of the coast on a trail the whole family will enjoy.

Distance: 3.0 miles out and back
Approximate hiking time: 1.5 hours
Elevation gain: 40 feet
Difficulty: Easy
Trail surface: Dirt and sand
Best season: Year-round

Other trail users: None
Canine compatibility: Dogs not permitted
Fees and permits: None
Trail contact: Montana de Oro State Park, 1 Pecho Valley Road, Los Osos, CA 93402; (805) 528-0513 or (805) 772-7434

Finding the trailhead: From the intersection of Marsh and Higuera Streets, head west on Marsh under the US 101 freeway, taking the ramp onto US 101 South. Drive for 0.2 mile and exit at CA 227/ Madonna Road. Turn left onto Madonna Road and drive for 1.0 mile. Make a right onto Los Osos Valley Road and drive for 10.3 miles. Continue on Pecho Valley Road for 3.7 miles. Park at the Bluff Trail Trailhead. GPS Trailhead Coordinates: 35° 16' 22" N, -120° 53' 19" W

The Hike

The bluffs at Montana de Oro State Park create a spectacular display. Layer upon layer of eroding diatomic rock of the Monterey formation and sandstone have been marvelously sculpted by the sea. In many places the bluff formations resemble fingers stretching out into the ocean. These layers of rock have been uplifted by the same tectonic forces that created the volcanic plug domes that stretch from Morro

Bay to San Luis Obispo. The power of natural processes is overwhelming here, and anyone with an interest in science is sure to marvel at the forces that have infused this place with so much majesty.

Montana de Oro is a magical place, and this is perhaps the shining star in a brilliant constellation of hikes. It will probably be busy; there is almost never a time when someone isn't present here. The Bluff Trail is without a doubt the most frequently traveled trail in the park, but the ocean breeze is clear and effervescent. If the time of year is right, meaning early spring through early summer, fields of gold will act as a natural accompaniment blanketing the hillsides. Here, tide pools can be observed, beaches can be enjoyed, the crashing force of the ocean dashes upon the fingerlike outcroppings of rock, raptors of many different feathers float by overhead—the accumulated beauty is simply mesmerizing. Sunsets are enchanting, and full-moon hikes can be supernatural.

From the parking area, head west along the trail across a bridge. Veer right at the split, walking along the bluff top, with a view into Spooner's Cove. The trail then begins to skirt the edge of the ocean and continues in a southerly direction until reaching a fence on the border of PG&E property. Just to the south is Diablo Canyon Nuclear Power Plant. At this point hikers must turn around and return via the same route or feel free to explore other trails in the area. It is possible to connect to the Coon Creek Trail by heading inland at this point along a connector trail that leads to the Coon Creek trailhead and the newly opened Diablo Power Plant Buchon Trail via the security gate. There are a variety of routes that lead through washes and up to the top of summits as well.

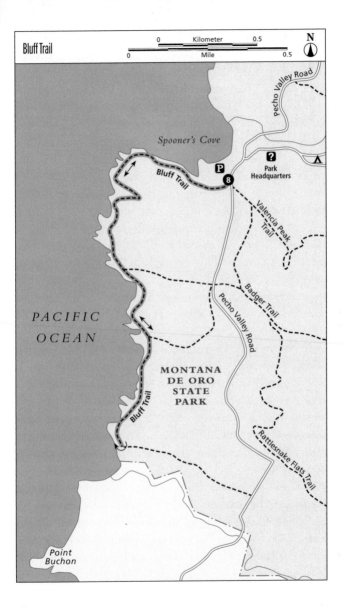

Bluff Trail

Kilometer
0   0.5
Mile
0   0.5

N

Spooner's Cove

Bluff Trail

P

8

Park
Headquarters

Valencia Peak
Trail

Badger Trail

PACIFIC

OCEAN

Pecho Valley Road

**MONTANA
DE ORO
STATE
PARK**

Bluff Trail

Rattlesnake Flats
Trail

Pecho Valley Road

*Point
Buchon*

Miles and Directions

0.0 From the parking area walk south to the end and take the Bluff Trail.

0.02 Cross the wooden bridge.

0.04 Veer right at the split in the trail. Follow the trail south along the ocean.

1.5 Reach the boundary fence. Return via the same route.

3.0 Arrive back at the parking area.

9 Coon Creek

Hike along a lovely creek, exploring the riparian side of Montana de Oro State Park.

Distance: 4.5 miles out and back
Approximate hiking time: 2.5 hours
Elevation gain: 500 feet
Difficulty: Easy
Trail surface: Dirt
Best season: Year-round

Other trail users: None
Canine compatibility: Dogs not permitted
Fees and permits: None
Trail contact: Montana de Oro State Park, 1 Pecho Valley Road, Los Osos, CA 93402; (805) 528-0513 or (805) 772-7434

Finding the trailhead: From the intersection of Marsh and Higuera Streets, head west on Marsh under the US 101 freeway, taking the ramp onto US 101 South. Drive for 0.2 mile and exit at CA 227/Madonna Road. Turn left onto Madonna Road and drive for 1.0 mile. Make a right onto Los Osos Valley Road and drive for 10.3 miles. Continue on Pecho Valley Road for 4.8 miles to the large parking area for Coon Creek. GPS Trailhead Coordinates: 35° 15' 29" N, -120° 53' 15" W

The Hike

Montana de Oro State Park is filled with a variety of terrain; the riparian woodland alongside Coon Creek is simply another example of the park's diversity and beauty. From late February through early May, there should be quite a display of wildflowers along the trail and spread throughout the park. Sticky monkey flower, morning glory, hummingbird sage, Johnny-jump-ups, arroyo lupine, figwort, honeysuckle, and the ubiquitous orangish/golden California poppy are everywhere. Due to an extreme amount of

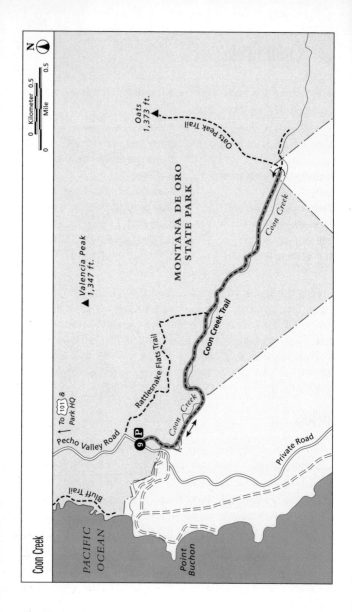

Coon Creek

PACIFIC OCEAN

Bluff Trail

Point Buchon

Private Road

Pecho Valley Road

↑ To 101 & Park HQ

Rattlesnake Flats Trail

Valencia Peak
1,347 ft.

Coon Creek

Coon Creek Trail

Coon Creek

MONTANA DE ORO
STATE PARK

Oats Peak Trail

Oats
1,373 ft.

N

0   Kilometer   0.5
0   Mile   0.5

moisture from coastal fog, mist, and a perennial stream, the trail seems more like a rainforest than a hike along California's Central Coast. Hanging moss and bracken dangle from the trees, and the undergrowth is thick and woody. Blackberries ripen on the vine and can be plucked and eaten raw by those who know what to look for.

From the parking/picnic area, head east along the Coon Creek Trail. The trail enters along the creek side after 0.25 mile. From there, it follows the verdant foundation of Coon Creek as it ascends gently toward the creek's source. There are multiple bridges along the way, six at least, so that hikers do not have to worry about wet feet. Watch for poison oak along this trail and snakes as well. The turnaround for the hike is the connector with the Oats Peak Trail at 2.25 miles, but hikers should feel free to explore for as long as they wish. The trail becomes overgrown farther upstream, but several options can be explored for those who want to take in all that Montana de Oro has to offer. Hikers wishing to make a grand loop can turn left onto the Oats Peak Trail and ascend 1.0 mile and 1,000 feet to a couple of marvelous summits and then head back to the coast and return via the Bluff Trail to the parking area. This adds quite a bit of distance to the overall hike and would give the hike a rating of difficult rather than easy.

Miles and Directions

- **0.0** From the parking area walk east and south along the Coon Creek Trail.
- **0.25** The trail enters the creek bottom, turns east, and climbs upstream.
- **2.25** Reach the Oats Peak Trail. Return via the same route.
- **4.5** Arrive back at the parking area.

San Luis Obispo City and County Open Spaces

Both the city and county of San Luis Obispo are filled with open spaces. Hiking, cycling, mountain biking, and equestrian endeavors are the norm. With the high population of students from Cal Poly San Luis and Cuesta College, the region is an outdoor haven. Outdoor spaces are located prominently throughout the region. Of the nine morros of San Luis Obispo County, three are located on open land operated by the city of San Luis and are accessible to the public.

Within the city proper no fewer than eleven sites are open to hiking and mountain biking. Outside of the city four large county parks provide excellent opportunities for outdoor excitement as well—all this in addition to the various state and national parks and forests that surround the region. Adventure awaits!

10 Eagle Rock Trail

Take a trip through the wild woodlands of El Chorro Regional Park and catch views of the nine morros and Eagle Rock.

Distance: 2.3-mile lollipop
Approximate hiking time: 1.5 hours
Elevation gain: 400 feet
Difficulty: Easy
Trail surface: Dirt, asphalt
Best season: Fall through spring
Other trail users: Dogs

Canine compatibility: Leashed dogs allowed
Fees and permits: Day-use fee per vehicle and per animal
Trail contact: San Luis Obispo County Parks, 1087 Santa Rosa St., San Luis Obispo, CA 93408; (805) 781-5930

Finding the trailhead: From the intersection of Marsh and Higuera Streets, head northeast on Marsh Street. Turn left onto Santa Rosa Street/CA 1. Drive for 2.3 miles. Continue onto CA 1 North/Cabrillo Highway/North Santa Rosa Street and drive for 3.6 miles. Turn right onto Dairy Creek Road and continue for 0.5 mile to the parking area. GPS Trailhead Coordinates: 35° 19' 52" N, -120° 43' 44" W

The Hike

El Chorro Regional Park was once made up of dairy farms and grazing lands. In the 1940s it was purchased by the federal government in order to create Camp San Luis Obispo. Here the army trained soldiers for thirty years. In 1972 President Richard Nixon turned the area over to San Luis Obispo County, where it has since been used for camping, softball, volleyball, a golf course, botanical gardens, and, of course, hiking. The open space is quaint, and the views are spectacular. This is a great hike for beginners and those with children. The trail gains elevation very steadily, but is short enough in duration that most people will find the walk exhilarating and not too tiring.

From the parking area, walk north for 0.2 mile up the road and through the pedestrian gate. Turn right and follow the self-guided nature trail. The numbered brochure can be picked up next to the gate. The brochures are provided by the Santa Lucia Chapter of the Sierra Club and should be returned upon exiting the trail. The signs are very easy to follow and will keep almost anyone on track. The stops on the trail are dedicated to plants, wildlife, and ecology such as poison oak, coyote bush, oak trees, mule deer, wood rats, birds, and vista points. A list of flowers is also provided for those who are keeping an eye out for them.

At 0.6 mile turn right and head to the Eagle Rock Viewpoint, which will be reached in less than 1.0 mile. From this spot, a fantastic panorama of the nine morros stretching from Morro Bay to Islay Hill south of the town of San Luis Obispo opens. For the small amount of work it takes to get there, it is definitely unmatched in splendor. At this point return back to the junction and turn right. Follow the trail through splendid elfin woodland. There is ample shade along the trail, so the jaunt is quite peaceful. At 1.8 miles the trail reaches Dairy Creek, which runs year-round. Once back at the road at 2.0 miles, turn left and follow the quaint sounds of the creek back to the parking area.

Miles and Directions

0.0 From the parking area follow the road north to the trailhead. Walk through the gated entrance and pick up a brochure.

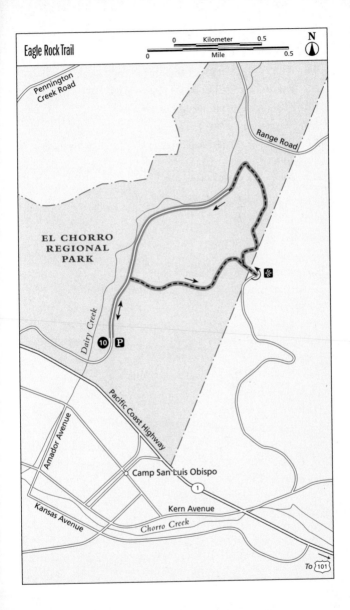

0.2 The self-guided nature trail begins on the right.

0.4 Follow the trail sign left.

0.6 At the junction turn right and head to Eagle Rock.

0.9 Reach Eagle Rock Viewpoint. Return to the trail junction.

1.2 At the junction take the trail on the right.

1.8 Reach Dairy Creek.

2.0 Reach Dairy Creek Road and turn left. Return to the parking area.

2.3 Arrive back at the parking area.

11 Bishop Peak

Take a hike to the top of the tallest of the nine morros of San Luis Obispo County and experience exhilarating views of the surrounding countryside.

Distance: 4.4 miles out and back
Approximate hiking time: 2.5 hours
Elevation gain: 1,200 feet
Difficulty: Moderate
Trail surface: Dirt
Best season: Year-round, hot in summer

Other trail users: Dogs, runners
Canine compatibility: Leashed dogs allowed
Fees and permits: None
Trail contact: City of San Luis Obispo Parks and Recreation, 990 Palm St., San Luis Obispo, CA 93401; (805) 781-7300

Finding the trailhead: From the intersection of Marsh and Higuera Streets, head northeast on Marsh and drive for 0.7 mile. Turn left onto Santa Rosa Street/CA 1 and drive for 1.0 mile. Turn left onto East Foothill Boulevard and drive for 0.9 mile. Turn right onto Patricia Drive and drive for 0.7 mile. Park alongside the road near the trailhead. GPS Trailhead Coordinates: 35° 18' 16" N, -120° 41' 07" W

The Hike

Bishop Peak tops out at 1,546 feet above sea level, making it the tallest of San Luis Obispo's nine morros. From the southern side, it is the third in a series of volcanic plug domes that picturesquely dominate the county skyline. The land was preserved and acquired through various donations and purchases and finalized as the Bishop Peak Natural Reserve in 1998. Bishop Peak is perhaps the most

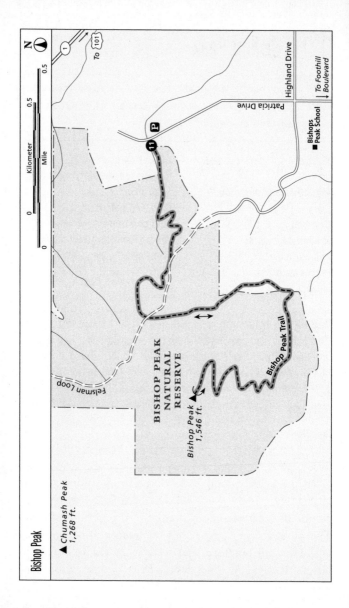

Bishop Peak

recognizable and frequently used of all the morros because of its ease of access, its size, and the variety of trails in the preserve. Towering above the northwestern end of the city, the peak was named by Spanish missionaries due to its apparent resemblance to a bishop's hat, or miter. It is easily identifiable from almost any nearby location.

The trail to Bishop Peak is well signed even though a variety of roads and trails intersect with the main route. When in doubt, watch for the signs and head toward the peak. From the Patricia Drive trailhead, hike west to a junction and trail sign at 0.2 mile, stay to the left, and continue on the Bishop Peak Trail. The trail switchbacks through oaken woodland a few times and reaches an old and often dry cattle pond at just about the 0.5-mile mark. Turn right and follow the trail through a gate and to another junction at 0.8 mile. Turn left at the junction. The trail remains quite forested through this section, skirting the base of the peak until reaching the old quarry site at 1.1 miles.

The trail is a fairly gentle climb until the 1.5-mile mark, making this an excellent training hike for larger and longer outings. The gentle beginning leads to a steeper finish at an optimal point in the hike, which will serve to build both muscle and stamina. At about this distance the trail intersects with several offshoots of the Old Bishop Trail, which once led steeply up Bishop Peak from Foothill Boulevard. Ignore them and continue straight around the upper base of the summit. From here the trail climbs more sharply, switchbacking to the lower section of the summit. Trails lead across the saddle to the three high points, and the summit blocks can be climbed with varying degrees of difficulty. Be careful with small children here, but take time to enjoy the views, which stretch across all of the nine sisters/morros from the gentle Pacific to Morro Bay. The surrounding countryside is truly beautiful, and the juxtaposition of countryside and developed land is a masterwork considering the state of much of Southern and Central California. There should be no doubt that this region is one of the most beautiful places on the earth. It should also be noted that Bishop Peak is a spectacular spot to catch a sunset. Sunrises aren't too shabby either.

Miles and Directions

0.0 Walk west along the trail toward Bishop Peak.

0.2 Veer left at the Bishop Peak Trail sign.

0.5 Turn right at the cattle pond.

0.8 Go through the gate and turn left at the junction.

1.1 Reach the old quarry site.

1.5 Stay straight on the main trail at several intersections with the Old Bishop Trail entering from the left.

2.2 Reach Bishop Peak. Return via the same route.

4.4 Arrive back at the trailhead.

12 Cerro San Luis

Climb to the top of the city of San Luis Obispo's most beloved mountain. Enjoy awe-inspiring views along a picturesque trail.

Distance: 4.75-mile lollipop
Approximate hiking time: 2–3 hours
Elevation gain: 1,350 feet
Difficulty: Moderate
Trail surface: Dirt
Best season: Year-round, hot in summer

Other trail users: Dogs, mountain bikers, runners
Canine compatibility: Leashed dogs permitted
Fees and Permits: None
Trail contact: City of San Luis Obispo Parks and Recreation, 990 Palm St., San Luis Obispo, CA 93401; (805) 781-7300

Finding the trailhead: From the intersection of Marsh and Higuera Streets, head west on Marsh under the US 101 freeway, turn right onto Fernandez Road, and park in the parking area. GPS Trailhead Coordinates: 35° 16' 30" N, -120° 40' 20" W

The Hike

Cerro San Luis, sometimes called Madonna Mountain, San Luis Peak, or San Luis Mountain, while not the tallest of the nine morros that dominate the San Luis Obispo countryside, is one of the more prominent. At 1,292 feet it is nearly 300 feet lower than its northern neighbor, but no less impressive, and the trails surrounding the peak are equally remarkable. While the peak and its environs are owned by the Madonna family of Madonna Inn fame, access to the peak is completely open due to the benevolence of the

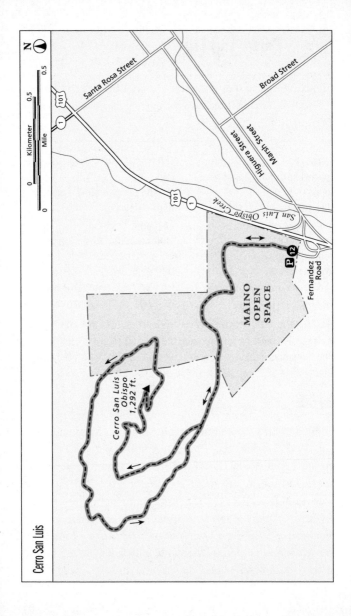

Cerro San Luis

proprietor. The painted white cement M on the eastern face stands for Mission High School, not the Madonna family as many mistakenly assume. Mountain-biking trails dominate the lower regions of the trail, and wide dirt roads snake their way around most of the mountain, including the path to the summit.

From the parking area, walk north along the main trail. Ignore the many smaller use paths and stay on the wide trail that leads to the base of the mountain. At just over 0.6 mile, in the entrance to a small canyon, veer left to stay on the main trail and avoid the use trail that leads to the M on the eastern face. Many smaller trails intersect after this point—staying on the widest path is the surest bet as well as the route that is followed here. At 1.0 mile the trail meets the well-graded road that climbs up to the summit. Follow it to the top. After enjoying the views, some hikers may wish to return via the same route, but to do so would be to deny the joy of a trip through the wooded northern face of the volcanic plug.

At the summit there is a smaller trail that leads east—clearly visible from the top, it is difficult to miss. From here the trail wraps around the northern face of the mountain, circumnavigating the entire base of Cerro San Luis. The route is easy to follow: Stay straight and ignore trails that enter from the right (north). There are multiple ways to access the open space of Cerro San Luis, and these trails are merely merging from other entrances to the park. At 3.75 miles the loop rejoins the trail back to the parking lot. Follow it back to the beginning.

Miles and Directions

0.0 Walk north from the parking area.

0.25 Follow the wide main trail as it turns west.

0.6 Continue straight and veer left at the mouth of a small canyon, ignoring smaller use paths on the right.

1.0 Continue straight onto the well-graded road that leads up to the summit.

2.0 Reach the summit of Cerro San Luis.

2.1 Take the small trail leading south and east around the northern flank of the peak. Follow the trail around the base, ignoring smaller trails entering from the right.

3.75 Arrive back at the junction with the road to the summit. Continue straight back to the parking area.

4.75 Arrive at the parking lot.

13 Reservoir Canyon

Hike through a riparian canyon past a lovely waterfall, oak woodlands, and a babbling stream in a lush and beautiful canyon.

Distance: 3.0 miles out and back
Approximate hiking time: 1.5 hours
Elevation gain: 400 feet
Difficulty: Easy
Trail surface: Dirt, asphalt
Best season: Fall through spring

Other trail users: Dogs, runners
Canine compatibility: Leashed dogs allowed
Fees and permits: None
Trail contact: City of San Luis Obispo Parks and Recreation, 990 Palm St., San Luis Obispo, CA 93401; (805) 781-7300

Finding the trailhead: From the intersection of Marsh and Higuera Streets, head west on Marsh, taking the ramp onto US 101 North. Drive for 3.1 miles. Turn right onto Reservoir Canyon Road and drive for 0.3 mile to the parking area. GPS Trailhead Coordinates: 35° 17' 29" N, -120° 37' 40" W

The Hike

Reservoir Canyon was protected as an open space due to its historic watershed value. The dry central California coast needed all the steady sources of water it could find. Water from the year-round creek was diverted into a reservoir by a private landholder, hence the canyon's namesake. Eventually the city bought the property, but when the city of San Luis Obispo began using the water from Santa Margarita Lake in 1947, the canyon became unimportant as a water supply. The city of San Luis Obispo held on to the land and

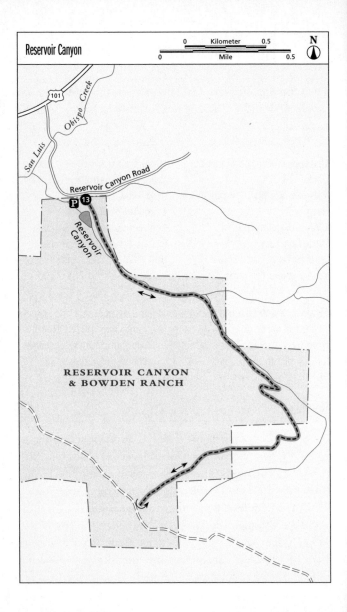

Reservoir Canyon

101

Obispo Creek

San Luis

Reservoir Canyon Road

P 13

Reservoir
Canyon

RESERVOIR CANYON
& BOWDEN RANCH

N

0   Kilometer   0.5
0   Mile   0.5

eventually turned it into an open-space park and preserve, free to the public and accessible for recreational use.

From the parking area, walk through the gate and begin hiking along the trail. A lovely arboreal canopy stretches overhead, and the trail feels quite a bit more remote than it actually is. The waterfall appears within 0.1 mile of the parking area. It just happens to be the tallest waterfall in San Luis Obispo County and after a rain can be quite impressive. However, the water level trickles off the dryer it becomes, though there is always some water, just not enough to be spectacular without very recent precipitation. From the waterfall continue upstream along a very gentle upgrade crossing many boardwalks and bridges. The sycamore/oak riparian woodland is beautiful and shaded, making it pleasant even on hotter days. Wildflowers are the norm and the trail is always lovely and peaceful, even with a high volume of use. The hike is a favorite of many in San Luis, especially after rains.

The trail follows the bottom of the canyon and enters into a lovely shady glade before eventually climbing up the mountainside for exquisite views of the city of San Luis Obispo and several of the nine morros. Hikers with lots of energy can take the trip to the top for the exercise and the views, or turn around and return via the same route to the parking area.

Miles and Directions

0.0 From the parking area cross the road and enter the trail through the gate.

0.1 View the waterfall. Continue along the trail.

1.5 Reach the turnaround point where the trail climbs up the grassy mountainside.

3.0 Arrive back at the parking area.

Los Padres National Forest

The Los Padres National Forest stretches from the eastern edge of Ventura County to the Ventana Wilderness north of Big Sur. The swath that cuts through San Luis Obispo County is broken by private landholdings in the coast ranges, and the elevation is generally lower than other parts of the forest.

Made up primarily of oak-covered rolling hills, the highest peak near the town of San Luis Obispo is Cerro Alto, and a fantastic hike to the summit is covered in this chapter. Two very fine waterfalls sit just a short distance off mountain roads within the boundaries of the Santa Lucia Wilderness. The forest is there to explore and enjoy, just be sure to bring along an Adventure Pass, which is required for parking anywhere within the Los Padres National Forest.

14 Cerro Alto

Take a trip to the highest vantage point along the West Cuesta Ridge, following a creek through the forest and gaining a viewpoint of most of San Luis Obispo County.

Distance: 4.25-mile lollipop
Approximate hiking time: 2.5 hours
Elevation gain: 1,600 feet
Difficulty: Moderate
Trail surface: Dirt
Best season: Year-round, hot in summer
Other trail users: Mountain bikers, dogs, runners

Canine compatibility: Leashed dogs allowed
Fees and permits: National Forest Adventure Pass required for parking, either daily or annually
Trail contact: Los Padres National Forest, 6755 Hollister Ave., Suite 150, Goleta, CA 93117; (805) 968-6640

Finding the trailhead: From the intersection of Marsh and Higuera Streets, head west on Marsh, taking the ramp onto US 101 North. Drive for 17.3 miles to exit 219 for CA 41/Morro Road. Turn left onto El Camino Real. Turn left onto CA 41 South/Morro Road and drive for 8.8 miles. Turn left onto Cerro Alto Road. Drive 1.0 mile to the campground and day-use parking. GPS Trailhead Coordinates: 35° 25' 29" N, -120° 44' 26" W

The Hike

Cerro Alto is one of the tallest coastal mountains near the city of San Luis Obispo. From atop its summit, unobstructed views reach far and wide, stretching from the blue of the Pacific, taking in all of the nine morros of San Luis, to the higher mountains farther inland in the Santa Lucia

Range. A large swath of San Luis Obispo County can be viewed from the peak's loftiest reaches, and no one should be disappointed with the vantage point.

The hike to Cerro Alto is one of the more challenging in this book, due to its elevation gain. Though the trail is never steep and actually graded fairly gently, it does climb 1,600 feet in 2.5 miles. Expect a cardio workout on this trail, especially if keeping a quick pace.

From the campground and day-use area, take the signed trail from the day-use parking lot. This trail is gentler, starts off with a more level climb, and is the longer section of the loop, spreading the climb out over a larger distance. Head east along Morro Creek, which will intermittently be wet in places during dry times and pretty and flowing during rainier times of the year. Here the trail follows the canyon carved out by the creek and meanders through pretty oak woodland for the better part of a mile. At 0.9 mile turn sharply right and follow the access road west through open grassland around the northern base of the peak.

At 1.6 miles turn left onto the narrower route up to the summit. This portion of the trail follows a completely open, sun-exposed hillside that is almost always either being totally blasted by coastal winds or completely devoid of even the gentlest of breezes—hikers should be prepared for either extreme. The trail can be desiccating and hot or bone chilling at almost any time of year. At 2.0 miles and another intersection, turn left again, making the final push to the summit and ignoring any other side trails on your right. Some remnants of the old lookout tower still exist to explore, but most will want to simply enjoy the views.

The return loop follows the path back to the junction encountered originally at 1.6 miles. Turn left at this

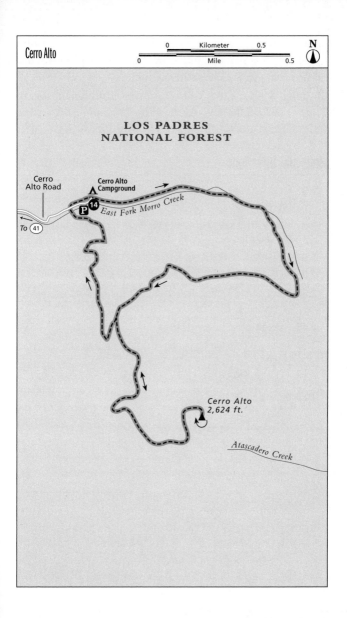

intersection 3.45 miles into the hike and follow the road for 0.1 mile to a signed trail junction. While there is some shade on this route, it is clearly less forested than the other side of the loop, steeper, and a favorite of local mountain bikers. The route leads back to Cerro Alto Road. Turn right and walk the remaining 0.1 mile to the day-use parking area.

Miles and Directions

0.0 From the day-use parking area, head east along Morro Creek.

0.9 Turn sharply right and head west back around the base of the summit.

1.6 Turn left and ascend the narrower path to the peak.

2.0 Turn left and stay on the trail to the summit.

2.55 Arrive on the summit. Return to the intersection encountered at 1.6 miles.

3.45 Turn left at the intersection.

3.55 Turn right onto the signed trail to return to Cerro Alto Campground.

4.15 Turn right onto Cerro Alto Road.

4.25 Arrive back at the day-use parking area.

15 East Cuesta Ridge

Take a walk along the crest of East Cuesta Ridge to the summit of Mount Lowe.

Distance: 7.0 miles out and back
Approximate hiking time: 4 hours
Elevation gain: 1,150 feet
Difficulty: Moderate
Trail surface: Dirt, gravel
Best season: Fall through spring
Other trail users: Dogs, mountain bikers, runners

Canine compatibility: Leashed dogs allowed
Fees and permits: National Forest Adventure Pass required for parking, either daily or annually
Trail contact: Los Padres National Forest, 6755 Hollister Ave., Suite 150, Goleta, CA 93117; (805) 968-6640

Finding the trailhead: From the intersection of Marsh and Higuera Streets, take US 101 North for 7.1 miles to Cuesta Pass. Just after the sign is Mount Lowe Road/Forest Route 30S11. Park safely along the freeway/Mount Lowe Road, but do not block the road. GPS Trailhead Coordinates: 35° 20' 59" N, -120° 37' 53" W

The Hike

Cuesta Ridge is discernible from almost anywhere in the San Luis Obispo region as the front crest line of the Santa Lucia Mountains, protecting the coastline from the heat of the central valley and standing above the city like sentinels behind the morros. Hiking or biking along the ridge involves travel along the dirt Mount Lowe Road, Forest Road 30S11.

From the roadside parking area, climb over the locked gate and ignore the NO TRESPASSING signs. It may seem like the area is restricted, but the gate is locked to prevent motor vehicles from using the roadway. The area is most assuredly

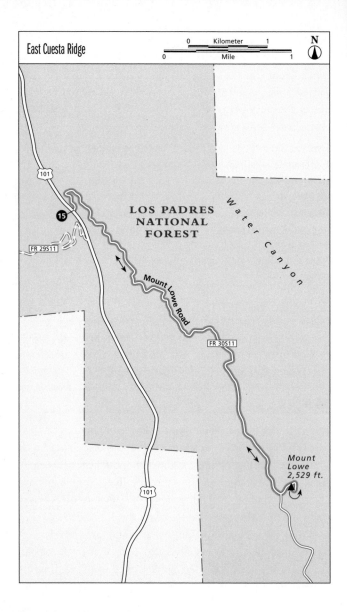

East Cuesta Ridge

Kilometer

Mile

N

101

15

FR 29S11

LOS PADRES
NATIONAL
FOREST

Water Canyon

Mount Lowe Road

FR 30S11

101

Mount
Lowe
2,529 ft.

open to bicycle and pedestrian traffic; the signs just have not been removed. The road climbs steadily for the first mile and a half, gaining 500 feet of elevation in that distance. At that point the road joins the ridge. Turn right and follow the road along the ridgeline, taking in fantastic views in all directions. Although hiking along a road may not seem like the most interesting of trecks, the views are unmatched. Walking atop a mountain ridge is an experience like no other; the views become an intensely integrated part of the trip. In the summer, morning coastal fog can sock in the entire coast, giving the mountains an ethereal feeling similar to floating in the clouds. When not closed in by fog, the views reach up and down the coast with an excellent vantage point of the nine morros of San Luis Obispo and the Pacific Ocean.

Follow the road as it climbs and leads prominently toward Mount Lowe. Mount Lowe is easy to spot because of the communication towers perched atop its summit. At 3.4 miles turn left and ascend to the towers. From atop Mount Lowe, one can peer into the city of San Luis and back across the wilderness to the east. Follow the road back to the parking area and enjoy a different perspective of the open views of the surrounding countryside on the return voyage.

Miles and Directions

0.0 From the parking area climb over the locked gate and walk up the road.

1.5 At the junction turn right and follow the road along the crest toward Mount Lowe.

3.4 Turn left and walk up the road to the towers atop Mount Lowe.

3.5 Arrive atop Mount Lowe. Return via the same route.

7.0 Arrive back at the parking area.

16 Big Falls

Walk through a lovely wooded canyon past two magnificent waterfalls and lots of pools just perfect for an afternoon swim.

Distance: 2.0 miles out and back

Approximate hiking time: 1 hour

Elevation gain: 400 feet

Difficulty: Easy

Trail surface: Dirt, rock

Best season: Late fall through early spring

Other trail users: Dogs

Canine compatibility: Leashed dogs allowed

Fees and permits: National Forest Adventure Pass required for parking, either daily or annually

Trail contact: Los Padres National Forest, 6755 Hollister Ave., Suite 150, Goleta, CA 93117; (805) 968-6640

Finding the trailhead: From the intersection of Marsh and Higuera Streets, head west under the freeway and onto US 101 South and drive for 14.7 miles. Take the CA 227/Grand Avenue exit. Turn left onto CA 227/Grand Avenue and drive for 1.0 mile. Turn right onto Huasna/Lopez Road and drive for 9.7 miles. Turn right onto Hi Mountain Road and drive for 0.8 mile. Make a slight left onto Upper Lopez Canyon Road and drive for 6.5 miles. Turn right and stay on Upper Lopez Canyon as it becomes a dirt road. The road is rough, with several creek crossings. At times the road is very wet. Four-wheel drive and high clearance are recommended. Drive for 3.5 miles to the trailhead on the left. GPS Trailhead Coordinates: 35° 15' 37" N, -120° 30' 48" W

The Hike

Big Falls Canyon is one of the premiere hiking destinations in San Luis Obispo County. Not one but two striking waterfalls can be seen on this hike, and some easily accessed swimming holes are just part of the fun. Visitors will not be disappointed when venturing here after steady rainfalls, though in dryer years and toward the middle to end of summer, there really isn't much water to go around. Often, during the rainy part of the year, the water is quite cold and not suitable for swimming except for the most daring of souls, but there are those wonderful hot spring days when conditions are perfect for diving in and cooling off.

Driving to the trailhead is a tough proposition without a high-clearance vehicle and four-wheel drive, though it is possible to make it if one has the gumption and patience to do so with care. It is not recommended, however.

From the parking area alongside the road at the trailhead, walk north up the canyon. The trail is gentle and not very steep as it climbs through the lush riparian and oaken canyon. The route is easy to track as there is really no way to go but to follow Big Falls Creek. At 0.4 mile the lower falls appear. They are a grand sight when in full pour. A large pool fills below the 30-foot cascade, and this is a great place for swimming if the temperature is right. An even larger pool sits just above the falls higher up the trail. The trail persists upstream and continues to climb at a gentle pace for another 0.6 mile. Here the second set of falls comes into view. This waterfall is more than twice as tall as the lower set, but it is substantially thinner and contains less water. It is less visited than the lower falls, but the pool that gathers underneath is equally good for swimming. Many rock pools line the creek and all are open to swimming.

The trail continues another 1,000 feet and a mile or so up to the ridgeline, but the journey outlined in this book stops here. Visitors should return via the same route to the parking area.

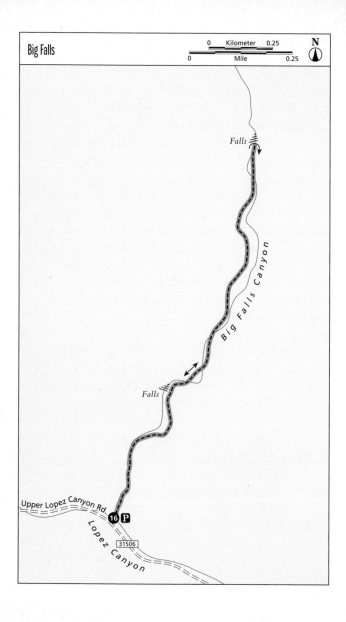

Big Falls

Falls

Big Falls Canyon

Falls

Upper Lopez Canyon Rd.

16 P

31506

Lopez Canyon

N

0   Kilometer   0.25
0   Mile   0.25

Miles and Directions

0.0 From the roadside parking area, walk north along the trail.

0.4 Arrive at the lower waterfall.

1.0 Arrive at the upper waterfall. Return via the same route.

2.0 Arrive back at the parking area.

17 Little Falls

Stroll through a sylvan canyon to a magnificent 50-foot waterfall.

Distance: 1.0 mile out and back
Approximate hiking time: 1 hour
Elevation gain: 300 feet
Difficulty: Easy
Trail surface: Dirt, rock
Best season: Late fall through early spring
Other trail users: Dogs

Canine compatibility: Leashed dogs allowed
Fees and permits: National Forest Adventure Pass required for parking, either daily or annually
Trail contact: Los Padres National Forest, 6755 Hollister Ave., Suite 150, Goleta, CA 93117; (805) 968-6640

Finding the trailhead: From the intersection of Marsh and Higuera Streets, head west under the freeway and onto US 101 South and drive for 14.7 miles. Take the CA 227/Grand Avenue exit. Turn left onto CA 227/Grand Avenue and drive for 1.0 mile. Turn right onto Huasna/Lopez Road and drive for 9.7 miles. Turn right onto Hi Mountain Road and drive for 0.8 mile. Make a slight left onto Upper Lopez Canyon Road and drive for 6.5 miles. Turn right and stay on Upper Lopez Canyon as it becomes a dirt road. The road is rough, with several creek crossings. At times the road is very wet. Four-wheel drive and high clearance are recommended. Drive for 1.6 miles to the trailhead on the left. GPS Trailhead Coordinates: 35° 14' 45" N, -120° 29' 16" W

The Hike

The falls at Little Falls Creek are not quite as impressive as the neighboring falls just down the roadway at Big Falls, but they are just as fun and a bit easier to reach. Driving to the trailhead is a tough proposition, though, without a high-clearance vehicle and four-wheel drive. It is possible to make it if one has the gumption and patience to do so with care. Also, the distance one has to drive on rough road is less than half of that to the Big Falls trailhead.

As with Big Falls, visitors will not be disappointed when venturing here during the rainy season. Though in dryer years and toward the middle to end of summer, there really isn't much water to go around. A drawback to both hikes along Lopez Canyon is that during the rainy part of the year, the water is quite cold and not very suitable for swimming except for the most daring and unflinching of souls. Epicureans, ice swimmers, and barbarians will delight in the fresh chill, but for most it will be quite off-putting. The scenery is beautiful enough just for looking, but there are always those wonderful hot spring and early summer days when conditions are perfect for simply diving in and cooling off.

Fern-lined, cool, riparian, and beautiful, the hike itself is stunning and the wildflowers are gorgeous. The walk is very short and gentle; in just under 0.5 mile, the trail gains only 200 feet before reaching the brief side trail on the left that wanders to the falls. Reminiscent of some other Southern California falls, such as Nojoqui, Rose Valley, and Limekiln Falls, the limestone falls drop and drip over 50 feet into a shallow pool below. The pool at the base of the falls is not the greatest for swimming, but farther along the main trail, there are an ample amount of wonderful pools for those who want to go for a dip. Return via the same route.

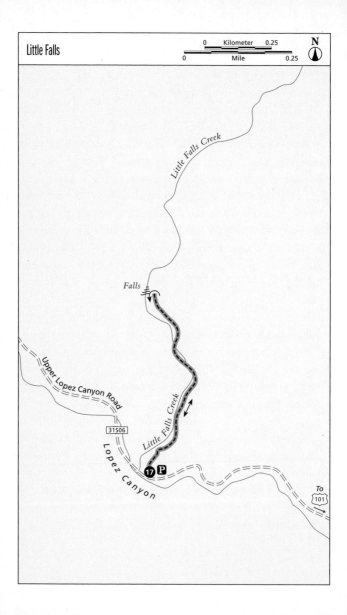

Little Falls

Miles and Directions

0.0 From the parking area alongside Upper Lopez Canyon Road, head north along Little Falls Trail.

0.49 Turn left onto the small use trail and walk toward the falls.

0.5 Arrive at Little Falls. Return via the same route.

1.0 Arrive back at the parking area.

18 Grey Pine Trail

Take a stroll beneath towering pine forest and looming grass–covered hills overflowing with sandstone beside lovely Santa Margarita Lake.

Distance: 5.2 miles out and back

Approximate hiking time: 3 hours

Elevation gain: 800 feet

Difficulty: Moderate

Trail surface: Dirt

Best season: Year-round, very hot in summer

Other trail users: Dogs

Canine compatibility: Leashed dogs allowed

Fees and permits: None

Trail contact: San Luis Obispo County Parks, 1087 Santa Rosa St., San Luis Obispo, CA 93408; (805) 781-5930

Finding the trailhead: From the intersection of Marsh and Higuera Streets, head west onto US 101 North and drive for 9.6 miles. Take exit 211 to merge onto CA 58 East/El Camino Real. Drive for 1.7 miles. Turn right onto CA 58 East/Estrada Avenue and drive for 0.3 mile. Turn left onto CA 58 East/J Street. Drive for 1.3 miles. Continue on West Pozo Road for 6.4 miles. Make a slight left onto Santa Margarita Lake Road and drive for 1.1 miles. Turn right and park in the day-use parking area. GPS Trailhead Coordinates: 35° 19' 28" N, -120° 29' 32" W

The Hike

Santa Margarita Lake sits just twenty minutes outside of San Luis Obispo, nestled between the Santa Lucia Range and the La Panza Range. The reservoir is the main supplier of water for the city of San Luis Obispo so skin contact is absolutely prohibited. In other words, there is no swimming allowed, although many other recreational activities abound such as hiking, biking, boating, fishing, horseback riding, kayaking, and sailing. Close to the national forest but administered by the County of San Luis Obispo, the lake rests in a beautiful oak-filled valley with mountains rising up on either side. Quite frankly, the scenery is stunning and well worth the drive. The contrast of the hillsides with the cool blue of the lake makes for a hiking experience that is not to be missed.

The hike is named for the gray, or digger, pine tree and many of the trees can be spotted along the hike, though the surrounding woodlands are primarily made up of several varieties of oak. From the campground, walk south along the well-trodden trail. The route loops around and crosses several four-wheel-drive roads along the way, climbs to a magnificent overlook atop Eagle View, descends to White Oak Flat, and ends on the peninsula at Vaca Flat overlooking a thin section of Santa Margarita Lake on three sides. The trail is easy to follow, wide in most places and quite tranquil, despite the noise of boats. Santa Margarita is not the largest lake in the region, so it is not the busiest either. Midweek excursions are quite a bit more placid. Either way the scenery is amazing and worth every effort. Visitors will enjoy the views and the unique design of the cone of the digger pine. The oaken forest is rather lovely, with tall canopies ranging overhead for much of the voyage.

Those who desire a shorter hike can cut the distance in half by traveling only to Eagle View and back. Those wishing to make the hike into a point-to-point venture can park a car at White Oak Flat and join up farther down the trail.

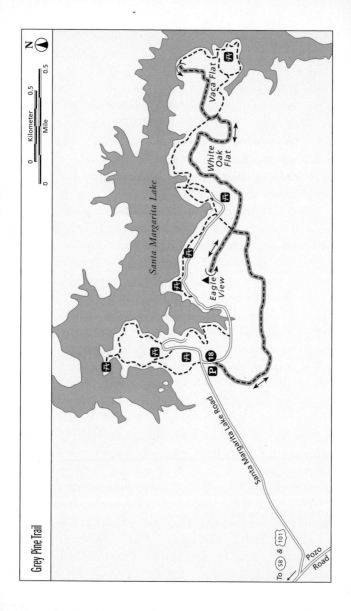

Grey Pine Trail

Santa Margarita Lake

Vaca Flat

White Oak Flat

Eagle View

Santa Margarita Lake Road

Pozo Road

To 58 & 101

N

0   0.5   Kilometer
0   0.5   Mile

P
18

Miles and Directions

0.0   From the parking area walk south along the trail.

0.4   Cross the road and continue along the trail.

0.5   Ignore the trail junction to the left and continue straight.

0.7   Ignore another trail junction to the left and continue straight.

1.1   Turn left onto the trail for Eagle View.

1.25 Arrive atop Eagle View. Return to the trail junction.

1.4   Continue straight on the trail to White Oak and Vaca Flats.

2.0   Arrive at White Oak Flat.

2.75 Arrive at Vaca Flat. Return via the same route.

4.1   Ignore the trail to Eagle View and continue along the trail to the Grey Pine parking area.

5.2   Arrive back at the parking area.

Carrizo Plain National Monument

Carrizo Plain National Monument was desig-
nated a national monument in 1991 and is
managed by the Bureau of Land Management.
It is the largest remaining native grassland in California
and the most undisturbed section of the San Joaquin
Valley ecosystem. At over 250,000 acres, the monument
protects habitat for several endangered plant and animal
species including the San Joaquin kit fox, the giant kan-
garoo rat, the San Joaquin antelope squirrel, the California condor, and the California jewelflower. Pronghorn
antelope and tule elk have been reintroduced to the area
by the Department of Fish and Game. Carrizo Plain
National Monument is one of the newest sites managed
by the National Park Service and the Bureau of Land
Management. It is also one of the least publicized. The
region is known for its brutal summer temperatures and
its lack of access during wet weather. However, through
late winter and spring, it is a veritable wonderland of
wildflowers and wildlife.

There are quite a few places of interest in the Carrizo
Plain, most notably the San Andreas Fault, which runs
straight through the eastern edge, where its scarring can be
seen directly upon the earth. This is the spot where science
textbooks get their pictures of fault lines. Archaeologically,

the plain holds some of the oldest relics of the Chumash Indians, including an incredible display of pictographs at Painted Rock. Despite weathering, erosion, and graffiti (from the 1800s to near present), the rocks remain some of the best examples of Chumash pictographs in California. Soda Lake is a massive saltwater lake that attracts migrating birds and strange plant life. Due to its saltiness, the land in this area was not as desirable as the much more fertile land to the north, and thus the lake is directly responsible for this parcel of land being preserved.

19 Painted Rock

Trek the Carrizo Plain among ancient Native American relics dating back 3,000 years.

Distance: 1.5 miles out and back
Approximate hiking time: 1 hour
Elevation gain: 300 feet
Difficulty: Easy
Trail surface: Dirt
Best season: Year-round, but access is limited from March 1 through July 15—only guided tours allowed during that time to protect nesting raptors
Other trail users: Dogs
Canine compatibility: Leashed dogs allowed
Fees and permits: None
Trail contact: Carrizo Plain National Monument, Bureau of Land Management, 3801 Pegasus Dr., Bakersfield, CA 93308; (661) 391-6000

Finding the trailhead: From the intersection of Marsh and Higuera Streets, head west onto US 101 North and drive for 9.6 miles. Take exit 211 to merge onto CA 58 East/El Camino Real. Drive for 1.7 miles. Turn right onto CA 58 East/Estrada Avenue and drive for 0.3 mile. Turn left onto CA 58 East/J Street. Drive for 1.3 miles. Turn left at Blue Star Memorial Highway/CA 58/Calf Canyon Highway and drive for 38.8 miles. Turn right at Blue Star Memorial Highway/CA 58 East/Carrisa Highway and drive for 3.0 miles. Turn right onto Soda Lake Road. Drive for 15.0 miles to the Painted Rock Visitor Center and Trail on the right. Turn right to drive to the visitor center, then left on the dirt road, and follow it 2.0 miles to the trailhead parking. GPS Trailhead Coordinates: 35° 08' 52" N, -119° 51' 42" W

The Hike

The Carrizo Plain contains one of the finest examples of ancient Chumash rock art. Archaeologists date the site to between 2,000 and 3,000 years old. Painted Rock itself is a towering mass looming over 50 feet high with a semicircular opening approximating the nearest thing to an outdoor church. The interior circle feels like the raised vertical nave of a cathedral. More than likely, there is more to this semblance, as there is no doubt to the sacred nature of this site. It is protected and still considered to be a holy place for the Chumash tribe. Being in the presence of such a site is magnificent. Strangely enough, it seems possible to feel the energy that flows through the air, as if the otherworldly power of the place is palpable. As is the rule with any artwork, don't touch or otherwise deface the pictographs—these are ancient holdovers from another time, and erosion and weather have taken a toll besides the damage done by humanity.

From the parking lot, walk gradually uphill to the south and follow the trail about 0.75 mile to the rock formation. The gentle slope is easy and even the smallest children should be able to handle the walk. It is impossible to wander off the trail or get lost. However, there are definite hidden dangers as rattlesnakes are ubiquitous in the monument. Due to hot, dry temperatures and the abundant presence of rodents such as ground squirrels, the reptiles thrive in this environment. There are warning signs all over the place, so please be wary and take care when bringing children to the monument. Biting and stinging insects can also be burdensome at certain times of the year, but they are not normally a problem. Visitors will return via the same route.

The artwork at Painted Rock is red and black; it varies from sun disks to animals to anthropomorphic figures. Some of the contrasts are strikingly beautiful; the red on black is quite artful and stunning. The site is still used for religious

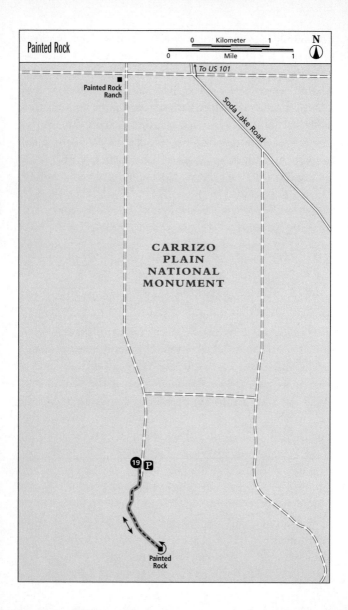

ceremonies during summer solstice, and the trail is closed from March 1 through July 15 to protect nesting bird species. Visitors to the monument can take guided tours with a park ranger only on Saturdays during that time. Some visitors are sure to enjoy the historic graffiti that dates back to 1870. Anything over fifty years old cannot be removed due to historical significance, though foolish people still continue to deface the monument every year. Violators can be punished with a $250,000 fine and up to two years in prison.

Miles and Directions

0.0 From the parking area head south along the trail.

0.75 Reach Painted Rock. Return via the same route.

1.5 Arrive back at the parking lot.

About the Author

Allen Riedel is a photographer, journalist, author, and teacher. He lives with his wife, Monique, and children, Michael, Sierra, and Makaila, in Riverside, California. He writes an outdoors column for the *Press Enterprise* and has authored several hiking guides, including *Best Hikes with Dogs in Southern California, 100 Classic Hikes in Southern California, Best Easy Day Hikes Riverside, Best Easy Day Hikes San Bernardino, Best Easy Day Hikes San Gabriel Valley, Best Easy Day Hikes San Diego,* and *Best Easy Day Hikes South Bay.*

WHAT'S SO SPECIAL ABOUT UNSPOILED, NATURAL PLACES?

Beauty Solitude Wildness Freedom Quiet Adventure
Serenity Inspiration Wonder Excitement
Relaxation Challenge

There's a lot to love about our treasured public lands, and the reasons are different for each of us. Whatever your reasons are, the national **Leave No Trace** education program will help you discover special outdoor places, enjoy them, and preserve them—today and for those who follow. By practicing and passing along these simple principles, you can help protect the special places you love from being loved to death.

THE PRINCIPLES OF **LEAVE NO TRACE**

- Plan ahead and prepare
- Travel and camp on durable surfaces
- Dispose of waste properly
- Leave what you find
- Minimize campfire impacts
- Respect wildlife
- Be considerate of other visitors

Leave No Trace is a national nonprofit organization dedicated to teaching responsible outdoor recreation skills and ethics to everyone who enjoys spending time outdoors.

To learn more or to become a member, please visit us at www.LNT.org or call (800) 332-4100.

Leave No Trace, P.O. Box 997, Boulder, CO 80306